Enid Blyton™

and her enchantment with

DORSET

Enid Blyton™
and her enchantment with
DORSET

DR ANDREW NORMAN

HALSGROVE

First published in Great Britain in 2005
Reprinted 2008. Revised 2010.

Copyright © 2005 Andrew Norman

Front cover *'Dorset's Isle of Purbeck'* by Linda Appleby.

Title page: *Enid Blyton.* Photo: Dorothy Wilding, reproduced with the
kind permission of Enid Blyton Limited, a Chorion company.

British Library Cataloguing-in-Publication Data
A CIP record for this title is available from the British Library

ISBN 978 0 85704 070 1

HALSGROVE
Halsgrove House,
Ryelands Industrial Estate,
Bagley Road, Wellington, Somerset TA21 9PZ
Tel: 01823 653777   Fax: 01823 216796
email: sales@halsgrove.com

Part of the Halsgrove group of companies
Information on all Halsgrove titles is available at: www.halsgrove.com

Printed and bound by SRP Ltd, Exeter

CONTENTS

FOREWORD

Visiting Dorset in July 2002, on a beautiful summer's day, and being driven round the countryside by Enid Blyton enthusiast, Vivienne Endecott, Gillian Baverstock, elder daughter of the late Enid Blyton, made the comment:

> We saw the Purbeck Hills, Studland Bay, Corfe Castle, Hartland Moor and had a beautiful drive over to Stourton Caundle. That countryside was part of my mother and her imagination.[1]

PREFACE

Enid Blyton first visited Dorset at Easter 1931 with her husband Hugh Pollock; she was aged thirty-four and pregnant for the first time. She would later return to spend many holidays in and around the town of Swanage in South Dorset's Isle of Purbeck, together with her two daughters: Gillian (born 1931) and Imogen (born 1935), and later with her second husband Kenneth Darrell Waters.

What was it about this particular region that would draw her back, time and time again, and what pursuits did she choose to follow whilst she was here? In order to find out, we accompany Enid as she walks, swims off Swanage beach, plays golf, takes the steam train to Corfe Castle, and the paddle-steamer to Bournemouth.

Although Enid's stories were drawn from her imagination, this itself was fed and nurtured by external experiences – in the case of 'The Famous Five' books, largely by what she had seen in Dorset. Whereas it is probably futile to attempt to match a specific real-life location with her fictitious ones, nevertheless it is a fascinating exercise to retrace her steps, and having done so, to reflect on those topographical features which might have impinged upon her subconscious (or what she called her 'under mind') whilst she was writing the stories. It is often the case that when an author bases his work on a certain place, the subsequent discovery by the reader of that place's true identity may come as a disappointment. Not so in this case, for the real-life locations are equally as interesting and exciting as the nail-biting adventures of 'The Famous Five' themselves!

'The Famous Five' books are treated chronologically, from the first, published in 1942, to the last in 1963. An account of Enid and her family, and in particular of their association with Dorset, runs concurrently.

Acknowledgements

Enid Blyton Ltd, a Chorion company; Hodder and Stoughton Ltd; ECC International, Europe; The Wedgwood Museum, Barlaston, Stoke-on-Trent, Staffs; Public Record Office, London; RN Submarine Museum, Gosport, Hants; HM Customs & Excise National Museum, Liverpool; *The Daily Mail*; *The Star*, Sheffield.

BBC South, Southampton, Hants; *Swanage and Wareham Advertiser*; *Daily Echo*, Bournemouth, Dorset; RNLI, Poole; Dorset Police, Winfrith, Dorchester; Corfe Castle Town Trust; Langton Matravers Local History and Preservation Society; Miss J. Barnard, The Blue Pool, Furzebrook, Wareham; Graham White, The Fox Inn, Corfe Castle; Isle of Purbeck Golf Club Ltd, Swanage, Dorset; The Friends of Bucknowle; The Corfe Castle Town Trust; Swanage Pier Trust; Purbeck Mineral & Mining Museum, Norden, Corfe Castle.

Imogen Smallwood, Dr David Aitken, George Willey; R.J. Saville; Barbara Stoney; Michael Ferguson; Dennis Smale; David Haysom; David Lewer; the late John Dean; Mrs Barbara Joan Rone; Mrs Barbara Haines; David Lewer, ARIBA; David Haysom; Nina McLaughlin; Michael Ferguson, Knoll House Hotel; C.D. Pike, OBE, DL; Oliver S.L. Simon; Frances Prescott; Jason Clarke; Susan Prust; John Rowley.

I am especially grateful to Gordon 'Johnny' James, and for the invaluable assistance given to me by Mrs Gillian Baverstock, who has helped me to rekindle something of the true spirit of Enid Blyton.

As always, I am indebted to my dear wife Rachel, for all her help and encouragement.

Author with Enid's eldest daughter,
Gillian Baverstock

ABOUT THE AUTHOR

Andrew Norman was born in Newbury, Berkshire, UK in 1943. Having been educated at Thornhill High School, Gwelo, Southern Rhodesia (now Zimbabwe) and St Edmund Hall, Oxford, he qualified in medicine at the Radcliffe Infirmary. He married in 1967 and has two children.

From 1972–83 Andrew worked as a general practitioner in Poole, Dorset, before a spinal injury cut short his medical career. He is now an established writer whose published works include biographies of Thomas Hardy, T.E. Lawrence, Sir Francis Drake, Adolf Hitler, Sir Arthur Conan Doyle, Agatha Christie and Robert Mugabe. Andrew remarried in 2005.

Details of Andrew Norman's books may be found on his website, www.andrew-norman.com

BOOKS BY THE SAME AUTHOR

Adolf Hitler: The Final Analysis
HMS Hood: Pride of the Royal Navy
By Swords Divided: Corfe Castle in the Civil War
Thomas Hardy: Behind the Inscrutable Smile
Tyneham: A Tribute
T.E. Lawrence: Unravelling the Enigma
Sir Francis Drake: Behind the Pirate's Mask
Dunshay: Reflections on a Dorset Manor House

Thomas Hardy: Christmas Carollings
Father of the Blind: A Portrait of Sir Arthur Pearson
Bournemouth's Founders and Famous Visitors
Jane Austen: An Unrequited Love
George Loveless and the Tolpuddle Martyrs
Agatha Christie: The Finished Portrait
Mugabe: Teacher, Revolutionary, Tyrant
Purbeck Personalities

APRIL DAY

Be silent, velvet bee,
  And let me brood
At peace in this enchanted loneliness.
  Chaffinch, take your merry song, and go
To some more distant tree.
  'Tis not my mood
To have this silence stirred
  By wing of bee
Or voice of bird.

By Enid Blyton

One

EASTER 1931:
ENID BLYTON VISITS CORFE CASTLE

Enid Blyton's first taste of Dorset occurred during the Easter of 1931, when she spent a holiday in Bournemouth (then part of Hampshire – now Dorset) with her husband Hugh Pollock. She was then aged thirty-three years. On 20 May, an article of hers was published by *Teacher's World* (a weekly journal designed for primary schools, to which she contributed). It describes how, during the course of that holiday, she made a visit to Corfe Castle in Dorset's so-called Isle of Purbeck (which in fact is not an island at all).

Approaching Corfe Castle.
Photo: Linda Appleby.

Her enchantment with the landscape is immediately obvious:

Dear Boys & Girls,

As I drove along in my little car I saw, far away, a rounded hill, and on it was the ruin of an old, old castle. I took the first road that led to it, and soon came to the hill. On the top were the remains of the castle itself. Round the slopes were the battlements with their slit-like windows. At the bottom of the hill was a deep ditch which once upon a time had held water and formed a moat all round the castle.

I sat down in the sunshine and looked up at the old ruin. How I wished I could see back through a few hundred years and know exactly what the castle had looked like when it was a real castle and not a ruin, when there were knights in jingling armour riding over the drawbridge, and when ladies in flowing robes walked to and fro on the grass beyond the battlements! I imagined a time when enemies rode against the castle and its owner, and when archers peered through the slit-like windows, and shot their deadly arrows downwards. I thought of what a dreadful time it must have been when gunpowder was used against the strong walls, and blew them to pieces, when for the last time weeping women hurried from their castle home, and strong men laid down their weapons and walked from the gates as prisoners. Then year by year the old place fell into ruin, and no longer was there the sound of laughing voices, the clank of armour or the neighing of horses.

'Now' I thought, 'the old castle is alone and forgotten. No one lives there, no one loves it' – but I was quite wrong; for suddenly I noticed hundreds of jackdaws sitting on the walls and squatting on the battlements. Then I heard their harsh voices as they quarrelled with one another or called to their mates. 'Chack!' they cried, 'Chack, chack!' I saw that in the walls there were hundreds of holes, where once upon a time timbers had rested to make floors and ceilings. In each hole there was a jackdaw's nest; there was not one I could see that had not a black and grey head peeping out from it. The castle had more creatures living in it and calling it their home than ever it had long ago.

Then a sandy rabbit popped out of a hole in the grass, just by my foot, and when he saw that I made no movement he frisked right by me. Out came others and still others, till a sudden clamour by the jackdaws and the flutter of wings frightened them and back they went again. 'Ha!' I thought, 'I was wrong! The old castle isn't a bit lonely or forgotten! It likes to dream by itself in the sun, and know that the jackdaws and rabbits love to be around it – maybe it likes them better than it does people, who bring guns and blow its granite walls and towers to bits!'

Now I must hurry back to the little car for I am on my way home, and I am longing to see Bobs and Sandy [her fox terriers] again and to fetch Pat and Bimbo [her cats] from the kennelman who is looking after them.

Much love to you all, from
Enid Blyton.[1]

What this letter reveals about Enid Blyton as a person, is her appreciation for, and love of nature. It also demonstrates her feeling for history, and a longing on her part to find out about the past. Finally, her writing displays an eloquence and beauty, bordering on the poetic.

In Dorset, and in the Isle of Purbeck in particular, were to be found such artefacts as castles, caves, cliffs, cottages, ships, dangerous rocks, a steam train, a golf club and a lighthouse. As will be demonstrated, these would feed her imagination with images which would later appear in one form or another in her 'Famous Five' series of books, and in *The Adventure of the Strange Ruby* (where some other children, not 'The Famous Five', holiday in Swanage and pause at Corfe Castle to buy lemonade).

By the time of her first visit to Dorset at Easter 1931, Enid had undergone a series of somewhat traumatic experiences, which she was obliged to endure and overcome before achieving success, fulfilment and happiness as a writer.

Two
FORMATIVE YEARS

The family home of Enid's parents, Thomas Carey Blyton (a cutlery salesman) and Theresa Mary (née Harrison, whose family was involved in the manufacture of steel cutlery forks) was Sheffield in Yorkshire.

However, Thomas's cutlery firm sent him to London, where he subsequently joined his two brothers in a firm belonging to their uncle which retailed Yorkshire cloth.[1] Thomas and Theresa's first home in the south was an apartment above a shop in Lordship Lane, Dulwich, Kent, and this is where, on 11 August 1897, their first child Enid was born.

From the earliest times, Enid and her father had a deep and loving relationship, and when, at the age of almost three months, Enid became dangerously ill with whooping cough, it was Thomas who sat up all night, cradling her in his arms, and 'willing her to stay alive.'[2] The following year, the family moved the 3 miles to Chaffinch Road, Beckenham. In 1899, their son Hanly was born; followed three years later, in 1902, by their second son Carey.

'From the time that she could walk,' said daughter Gillian, 'Enid accompanied her father everywhere.' He 'loved wild life and nature, and taught her everything he knew, giving her a knowledge and love of the subject which never left her.' (These were the early years of the twentieth century, Beckenham was surrounded by unspoilt country which they explored together.) Thomas was also a keen gardener, who 'helped her prepare her first patch of garden when she was five years old.' It was also he who instilled in Enid a love of poetry. 'My father used to quote poetry so often that it became part of my life,' said Enid.[3]

Left: *Thomas Carey Blyton – Enid's father.*
Photo: Emberson & Sons, Belgravia, London.
Right: *Theresa, Enid's mother (1924).*
Photo: Gillian Baverstock.

However, 'Enid had never got on very well with her mother, Theresa, who favoured her two sons, and insisted that Enid helped with the cooking and housework, while the boys were allowed to play. Her mother felt it was her duty to bring up her daughter to manage a home and family, and was particularly annoyed when her husband took Enid off to do other things.' It was clear therefore, that Enid was far more in tune with her father, than with her mother who took the traditional view that the woman's place was in the home. However, although Enid loved animals and longed for a pet… her father did not want a dog or cat spoiling his garden, and her mother felt exactly the same about having an animal in the house.[4]

There was another aspect of life about which Enid and her father disagreed. Thomas played the piano, and it was his ambition for his daughter to become a professional musician. To this end Enid, from the age of six, took piano lessons, the first of which her father gave her.[5] However, her abiding interest lay in reading. 'Enid was a very keen reader from a very early age,' said Gillian, who by the time she was aged ten, was borrowing books from the shelves of her father's extensive library.[6]

As a child, Enid went to church twice every Sunday, morning and evening, and to choir practice on Thursday nights. 'I went to Sunday school in the afternoon, and if there was a prayer meeting we stayed on for that too. Every year the Sunday School Union held a scripture exam, and I went in for it regularly,' she said.[7]

At the age of ten, Enid, having left her first school, was enrolled at St Christopher's School for Girls (private) in Beckenham, where she and two of her friends, Mirabel Davis and Mary Attenborough, started a magazine to which she contributed the stories.[8] (The school still possesses records of the debates in which she took part when in her teens.) 'I loved school,' she said, 'every minute of it. I loved learning. I never forgot what I had read. I can still shut my eyes and see a page of my geography book….' Enid was also fortunate in that her father possessed, 'hundreds of books of all kinds on every subject under the sun that interested him.' Here then was fodder aplenty to nurture her imaginative mind.

Enid also enjoyed the outdoor life, and used to play tennis and go cycling with her brother Hanly, who was two years her junior (but not so with Carey, who was five years her junior). 'My happiest childhood times were when I was reading and dreaming, when I was playing games with other children, and when I was out in the country or by the sea (possibly a reference to Scarborough in Yorkshire, which she visited when very young).'[9]

Sadly, there was a dark cloud on the horizon for: 'By the time Enid was twelve her parents were constantly arguing…,' said Gillian, so much so that: 'She [Enid] told stories to her younger brothers to distract them from the unpleasant quarrels that percolated upstairs.'[10] Matters finally came to a head when, 'after a tremendous row her father walked out.'[11] (In the same year Enid, then aged thirteen, was baptized at Elm Road Baptist Church.) When Theresa forbade the children from discussing the departure of her husband, 'Enid could not seek comfort from her friends.'[12]

Something of the pain experienced by Enid during those troubled years is reflected in her book, *The Six Bad Boys* (published 1951).

> That was a dreadful time for the three children [Hilda, Eleanor and Tom]. They had to cope with the tearful, complaining, angry mother, who had no idea where her husband was. They had to promise her not to tell anyone their father had gone away because of a row. They were to say he was on a visit. They had to face the fact that perhaps their father might never come back. 'I couldn't bear that,' said Hilda, wiping her eyes. 'Daddy wasn't so bad as mother always made out. She made him miserable.' 'We all made him miserable,' said her sister Eleanor. 'We were all miserable really. All that bickering and quarrelling! Dad's well out of it.' And then one day their mother had [received] a letter. 'He's made up his mind not to come back,' she said.[13]

> The ROW that night, was never forgotten. The three children were already in bed when it happened but they could hear the raised voices downstairs and they were frightened. Tom peeped into his sister's room. The light of the street lamp came through the window, and the boy saw the two girls kneeling beside their beds. He heard what Hilda was saying over and over again. 'Please God, let Dad come back. Please God, let Dad come back.'[14]

When Thomas went on to set up his own business as a clothing wholesaler, he continued to support his family and maintain contact with Enid. By now, 'he had met an intelligent woman who shared his love of books and music, which his wife had never done....'[15] This was Florence Agnes Delattre, a married woman who worked as a secretary in Thomas's uncle's cloth retailing company. As both Thomas's wife Theresa and Florence's husband refused to grant their respective spouses a divorce, the couple were unable to marry. Despite this, however, they went on to have a daughter Florence Carey, a son Gebir (whose name was later changed to Leslie), and another son who died aged six months.

Three

EARLY SUCCESS

Despite the trauma of her father leaving, Enid achieved success at school, where she excelled in both academic and sporting activities. Meanwhile, she derived encouragement in her writing, when in 1911, just before she attained the age of fourteen, she entered and won a poetry competition sponsored by journalist, editor, and writer Arthur Mee (1875-1943, producer of *The Children's Encyclopaedia* of 1908) in his weekly magazine. Much to her delight, he replied, 'You can write. Send in other things to our page. Perhaps one day you will REALLY write.' 'When my little poem was printed on the children's page in the magazine,' said Enid, 'I could have cried for joy!'[1] This success was to be short-lived when her stories and poems were, 'submitted and… rejected, piece after piece…'. Gillian believed the reason for this was that despite her young age, Enid was directing her efforts at the adult market.[2]

When the First World War commenced in 1914, Thomas was exempted from military service, being beyond the age for conscription. Enid's brother Hanly, however, served overseas with the army. Enid became head girl of her school. However, for her, the conflict between music and writing remained unresolved. 'When I was seventeen,' she said, 'I was spending four hours a day on music. I didn't want to. I wanted to spend more time on writing.'[3]

Having left school in 1915, Enid moved out of the family home to stay with her school friend Mary Attenborough in Beckenham. The next year was spent, 'studying singing, harmony, and piano. She passed her LRAM (Licentiate of the Royal Academy of Music) … and was offered a place at the Guildhall School of Music just before her nineteenth birthday.'[4]

In the summer of 1916, Enid was invited to stay at Seckford Hall, near Woodbridge, Suffolk, with the Hunt family (who were friends of Mary Attenborough's Aunt Mabel).[5] It was here that Ida, the Hunt's daughter, a trainee teacher at Ipswich Girls High School, discovered Enid's talent for telling stories to children. Ida therefore, 'suggested she [Enid] should take up teaching, and write during the holidays.' 'Quite suddenly,' said Enid, 'I knew what I ought to do. I knew it without a single doubt. I wanted to be a writer for children….[6] I would then be with children all day long, I would hear them talk, see things they did, find out exactly what they liked and disliked, what they feared, what they longed for. I would see naughty children and good children I would learn what the children wanted to read and also what they OUGHT to read!' This would later prove to be the secret of Enid's success, both in her fictional novels, and in the educational books which she would write for children.

The outcome was that in September 1916, Enid enrolled for the National Froebel Union Teacher Training Course, (named after the German, Friedrich Froebel, 1782-1852, who devised an educational system for kindergarten schools), joining Ida at Ipswich Girls' High School to teach children aged 7-14 years. The First World War ended on 11 November 1918. The following month, Enid duly qualified as a Froebel teacher and commenced work teaching juniors at Bickley Park Boarding School for Boys, Bromley, Kent.

In March 1919, Enid received her Teaching Certificate, with 'Distinctions in Zoology and Principals of Education; First Class grading in Botany, Geography, Practice of Education, History of Education, Child Hygiene, Class Teaching; Second Class grading in Literature and Elementary Mathematics.' However, having found that the responsibility of full-time teaching had left her with insufficient time for her writing, she departed a year later to take up the post of governess to the four sons of architect Horace Thompson and his wife Gertrude, who lived in nearby Surbiton.[7]

In 1920 Enid's father Thomas died suddenly of a stroke at the age of fifty. Her brother Carey now joined the Royal Air Force on a seven-year contract; whereas brother Hanly continued to live at home with his mother and took over the management of his father's business.

***

Having had several of her short stories and poems published in 1921, Enid achieved another breakthrough when in 1922, her first book *Child Whispers*, a collection of poems written for the Thompson boys and for other children who came to join her classes, was published by J. Saville and Co. of Gower

Enid aged twenty-six years.
Photo: Gillian Baverstock.

Street, London. In 1923, she commenced writing for the weekly journal *Teachers' World*.

Enid's early stories were about children and animals, and about fairies, pixies and brownies. Her father had given her books of traditional fairy stories; a subject dear to the heart of her paternal grandmother Mary Ann Hanly (the daughter of an Irish doctor), who also loved to recount tales of, 'great battles and brave deeds'. In fact it may have been Mary Ann who passed on to Enid, 'the way to tell a story, to make it come alive'.[8]

Four

MARRIAGE: A FAMILY

In 1923, Enid met Major Hugh Alexander Pollock, Head of Serial Publications at publisher George Newnes Ltd, when he and Enid were, 'discussing some educational nature books [of Enid's] which Newnes were to publish.' Hugh (born 29 July 1888), the eldest son of an antiquarian book seller from Ayr in Scotland, was a divorcee. Formerly a professional soldier, he had served in the First World War with distinction, and in 1919 was awarded the DSO (Distinguished Service Order).

Hugh commissioned Enid to write a book about London Zoo in 1924. On 28 April that year, the couple were married at Bromley Registry Office; none of Enid's relations were invited to the wedding.[1] Enid and Hugh's first home was an apartment in Chelsea, but they soon moved to a newly-built house in Shortlands Road, Beckenham, which they named Elfin Cottage. Here, they designed and made a garden, an occupation, 'which gave them great joy, and led to the publication by Enid of *Let's Garden'*. The couple were enjoying a happy marriage, and Enid's earnings from writing had risen from £300 in 1923, to over £500 a year.

In 1926, Enid became editor of a magazine for children entitled *Sunny Stories for Little Folk* (later known as *Sunny Stories*), published by George Newnes and costing twopence. Over the next ten years, a total of 250 volumes were produced. Newspapers to which Enid contributed during the 1920s and 1930s included: *The Morning Post, Child Education, Teachers' Times, The School Mistress, Punch, The Lady* and *Fairyland Tales*.[2] Also, since 1933, Enid had submitted articles and stories to the People's Dispensary for Sick Animals (PDSA), its junior division being known as the 'Busy Bees'.

In March 1927, Enid and Hugh purchased their first car, a Rover, and in the same year Enid, at Hugh's suggestion, purchased her first typewriter. 'By 1929 she [Enid] was writing a page containing schemes of work for teachers and stories for children,' said daughter Gillian. Enid now demonstrated what was to be a lifelong concern for sick children, by instigating a campaign whereby silver paper and foil were collected in order to raise money for Great Ormond Street Hospital.

In 1929 Enid and her household, including maid, nanny, and fox terrier 'Bobs' (soon to be famous!). moved to the appropriately named Old Thatch, a Tudor cottage with large garden and a well, situated in the more rural surroundings of Bourne End, Buckinghamshire, close to the River Thames. (Wells would feature in several of her subsequent books.) Hugh was a keen walker, and the couple enjoyed taking the car to interesting places, which they then proceeded to explore on foot. Enid's menagerie of pets (which she had been denied as a child) increased yearly, and now included (in addition to terriers Bobs and Sandy) pigeons, tortoises, cats and kittens. As for Bobs, he would soon become an author in his own right, and have his letters published in Enid's magazines!

Gillian, Enid's first child, was born on 15 July 1931. From that year, Enid and Hugh rented a furnished house on the Isle of Wight for their holidays.

During 1933, Hugh found himself increasingly busy in his capacity as editor at George Newnes, working for example with Conservative politician Winston Churchill on the latter's forthcoming book, *The World Crisis*. Having, as a serving soldier, witnessed the terrible carnage of the First World War, Hugh was subsequently subject to nightmares. After his monthly meetings with Churchill, who believed that another war was

highly likely, Hugh would return home seriously despondent. His general health was not good, and in that year, he and Enid spent a prolonged holiday in his native Scotland, in the hope that the rest would be beneficial. Meanwhile, Gillian was left in the care of her nurse.

Enid going shopping with Laddie.
Photo: The Topical Press Agency, Fleet St., London.

On 27 October 1935 (the year of King George V and Queen Mary's

Silver Jubilee), Enid's second child Imogen, was born. By now the family could afford a chauffeur-cum-gardener, a cook and a nanny. That November, Enid's beloved dog Bobs died and was buried in the garden.

The family moved yet again in August 1938, to Penn Road, Beaconsfield, Buckinghamshire, to a larger house with seven bedrooms and set in 2.5 acres of ground, which Enid named Green Hedges.

In 1939, Hugh met twenty-one-year-old Ida Crowe, who approached him with the manuscript of her first novel. (She would go on to have more than 200 novels published.) This meeting was to have severe repercussions for the future of his marriage to Enid. On 3 September, Britain and France declared war on Germany. Hugh, being beyond the normal age for military service, now joined the Home Guard.

The following year, 1940, Enid was to embark on a holiday in Dorset which would change her life, not only by giving her a deep and abiding love for that county, but also by inspiring her to write what is arguably her most memorable collection of books, namely 'The Famous Five' series.

Five

SWANAGE

In 1940, Enid visited the coastal town of Swanage in Dorset, together with her two daughters Gillian and Imogen. Perhaps it was the presence of her two children that inspired Enid to write the dazzlingly colourful and nail-bitingly exciting series of stories featuring three children, their cousin and a dog; for yes, 'The Famous Five' were shortly to make their appearance on the world stage! However, this time the atmosphere was entirely different from when Enid had visited Corfe Castle in 1931; the country was now at war, and had been since the previous September.

'It was March 1940 and I was eight years old,' said Gillian. 'I had been ill [with coughs and colds] and my mother had taken me away to Swanage in Dorset to get some sea air. We had never been to Swanage before....' The family stayed at The Ship Inn (Hotel) in the High Street where they shared a room, with Imogen, then aged five, sleeping in a cot.

'From there we went down to the beach to paddle and swim,' said Imogen. 'The inn was very old and reminded me of [my former home] Old Thatch.'[1]

Ship Hotel (in former times) with stone wagon.
Photo: David Haysom Collection.

In the spring of 1941 (by which time Hugh had officially rejoined the army), Enid took a holiday in Budleigh Salterton, Devon. Here she met, and fell in love with, fifty-year-old Kenneth Fraser Darrell Waters, a married man with no children who was separated from his wife. His background was as follows:

The son of a tax inspector, Kenneth had studied as a medical student at St Bartholomew's Hospital, London, before joining the Royal Navy as a surgeon lieutenant, and seeing action in the First World War at the Battle of Jutland. 'His ship was torpedoed twice,' he told Imogen, 'and the second time both his eardrums were blown out. This subsequently led to meningitis, and the resulting severe deafness caused him to be invalided out of the Navy.' When he met Enid, Kenneth was the senior surgeon at St Stephen's Hospital, Fulham Road, London.

Enid in her garden.   Photo: *Daily Graphic*

The allure of Dorset brought Enid and her two daughters back to Swanage in the summer of 1941, where this time they stayed in a boarding house at Marine Villas, The Parade (on the sea front). Here they were joined by Mabel Attenborough (the aunt of Enid's friend Mary who had taught her at Sunday school). Gillian describes the scene:

> Swanage was the centre of a pretty bay with chalk cliffs to the east, ending where the Old Harry Rocks stuck out into the sea. We could not walk along the cliffs to Studland at this time because it was out of bounds, or visit other places such as Lulworth that are further west along the coast. Somewhere near there was a lighthouse that we explored [Anvil Point].
>
> There were plenty of sunny days, though the wind blew most of the time. Our holidays had previously been spent on the Isle of Wight, but now it was war-time and we could not go there anymore. The seaside was strange at that time because the beaches were covered with iron scaffolding to stop German tanks coming ashore; while the shoreline was guarded by barbed wire and concrete pillars interspersed with

concrete pillboxes, where a watch was kept for an invasion fleet.

One day we took the train to the little village of Corfe, with its narrow, twisting street and small grey stone houses. In the middle of the village is a tall, green mound and on the top is the ruin of an old castle with the remains of a tower rising up, just off centre. We climbed the mound and found trees growing through the stones of the ruined courtyard, and heard jackdaws calling, 'Chack! Chack!' as we sat down out of the wind.[2]

For Enid and her children, visiting Swanage was not without an element of danger. They would surely have noticed the many buildings in the town that had been (and continued to be) damaged or destroyed by the bombs of the German Luftwaffe. 20 April 1942, for example, saw the bombing of Cornwall Road and Station Road, Swanage, with five killed and 21 wounded. On 14 May, a cottage where preacher and founder of Methodism, John Wesley had once spent a night (12/13 October 1774) was destroyed by enemy bombing. By this time there had been no less than 315 air-raid alerts in the town.

By 1941, 35 of Enid's children's books had been published, and she had commenced writing no less than eight series of books as follows: *Wishing Chair*, *Secret Island*, *Naughtiest Girl in the School*, *Adventurous Four*, *Enchanted Wood*, *Cherry Tree Farm*, *Mr Galliano's Circus* and *Twins of St Clare's*. 'The Famous Five' series, however, was yet to come! According to Gillian, although it was not Enid's habit to write whilst on holiday (apart from letters), nonetheless 'she enjoyed reading historical novels, Agatha Christie and light romances.'[3]

Six

FIVE ON A TREASURE ISLAND

The fact that Britain was at war did nothing to dampen Enid's spirits, and her desire to entertain, thrill and inform the increasingly large number of children who had become her avid readers and supporters.

Gillian recalls that Enid's first 'Famous Five' book – *Five on a Treasure Island* (published 1942) – was written about twelve months after her holiday with

the children in Swanage in March 1940. This was the first in a series of 21 'Famous Five' books – a new title being produced each year, with Dorset's Isle of Purbeck being the source of Enid's inspiration. 'I think that the things that we had seen down here somehow percolated into that book,' said Gillian, 'and I'm sure that Corfe Castle must have been the picture her [Enid's] imagination showed her of the castle on Kirrin Island.'[1]

Enid, who preferred to write outdoors, watched by Gillian and Imogen.

Photo: National Magazine Co., London.

Although Enid had seen Corfe Castle for the first time on her visit to Dorset in 1931, to her two daughters it was a novelty. One may imagine their excitement, as the train from Wareham crossed the viaduct on its approach to Corfe railway station, and Gillian and Imogen caught a glimpse of the towering Norman keep, crumbling yet still majestic, despite the passing of years.

Later, they travelled again by train to Corfe; this time from Swanage, through the undulating Dorset countryside, with its scattered hamlets and lush, green fields grazed by cattle and sheep, which burgeoned with wild flowers during springtime. Now they would have the added joy of climbing to the summit of the hill on which the castle stands, where jackdaws circled above them, and from where the quaint, stone-built village of Corfe Castle nestled below.

Just as the landscape percolated (as will be demonstrated) into Enid's sub-conscious so in her writing of 'The Famous Five' series of books, her own children were never far from her thoughts. For example, 'The reason that 'The Famous Five' always drank ginger beer,' said Gillian, 'was that it was my favourite drink as a child. Also, in those days, there was little choice!'

In *Five on a Treasure Island*, the reader is introduced to 'The Famous Five': Julian, Dick and Anne Kirrin, Georgina Kirrin (their cousin, known as 'George',) and Timmy her dog; also to 'Kirrin Island' and 'Kirrin Castle'. ('Kirrin Castle' also features in *Five on Kirrin Island Again*, published in 1947.)

Julian, Dick and Anne spend the summer holiday at the home of their Uncle Quentin, a scientist, his wife Fanny, and their daughter George, who is the same age as Dick. Quentin is a rather disgruntled character who writes books with such limited success, that Fanny is obliged to take in lodgers in order to supplement the family income. Quentin and Fanny live at Kirrin Cottage (in Kirrin village) which looks out over Kirrin Bay, a place ideal for bathing and rock climbing; the entrance to which is guarded by the rocky Kirrin Island. Their daughter Georgina (George) is an only child, who is very much of a tomboy and boasts that, 'she can climb better than any boy, and swim faster too.' [TI p.16.] Set on the top of the island is 'Kirrin Castle', described as, 'built of big white stones', with, 'broken arch-ways, tumbledown towers', and 'ruined walls'. Once, 'beautiful… proud and strong', the castle is now a home for jackdaws.

When she learns that Uncle Quentin has received an offer from a man who wishes to purchase Kirrin Island, and rebuild it as an hotel and holiday resort, George becomes angry, as she believes that her parents had given the island to her.

The children decide to make an excursion to the island, taking with them George's mongrel dog Timmy, but because he is not welcome with Uncle Quentin, Timmy resides with Alf, a 'fisher-boy' to whom George is obliged to pay all her pocket money for Timmy's upkeep. Here, they discover a map (plan) of Kirrin Castle, from the days before it was a ruin. By using the map, the children are able to identify the location of the dungeons, and the position of the steps leading down to them. (Timmy also proves his worth by inadvertently disappearing down a hole whilst in pursuit of a rabbit, thereby discovering the position of the castle's well!)

Having discovered the entrance, they raise the stone that covers it and climb down the steps into the dungeon, which is hollowed out of the rock itself. Finally, having broken down a large, heavy, interior door the children discover, 'brick-shaped things of dull, yellow-brown metal', which they realize are the ingots.[2] Suddenly the children discover that they are not alone. The prospective purchaser of the castle has arrived on the scene with two accomplices. They detain Julian and George, and send Timmy up to the surface with a note attached to his collar, where Dick and Anne have gone to get some fresh air, Dick having been wounded in the face by a wooden splinter while attempting to smash in the door with an axe. However, the note is signed 'Georgina', and this makes Dick suspicious, as this is a name which she hates, preferring the appellation 'George'.

After further dramas, the children manage to strand the three men on the island, while they make their escape in the rowing boat. To the children's relief, Uncle Quentin, at first sceptical of their story, finally accepts it and congratulates them, saying how proud he is of his daughter George, in particular. The story ends happily for everybody except the three villains, who are detained by the police. With the gold, Quentin tells George, I will now be, 'rich enough to give you and your mother all the things I've longed to give you for so many years and couldn't.' For George however, what she wants most in all the world is, 'to keep Timmy and have him here for my very own.' This, her father agrees to. As for Julian, Dick and Anne, George decides to give them a quarter-share each in Kirrin Island and its castle, which from henceforth, 'shall belong to us all!'[3]

Kenneth, the new love in Enid's life, joined her in Swanage for the first time in the summer of 1942 (with 'Auntie' Dorothy Richards present in the role of chaperone).[4] On 23 August, following several more air raids on the town and consequent loss of life, The Ship Hotel in the Square (the very place where Enid and her family had spent their holiday in March 1940) was bombed, resulting in the destruction of its west wing, and the loss of five lives and nine wounded.

Seven

CORFE CASTLE

orfe Castle stands on a promontory on the main chalk ridge of hills
which runs across the Isle of Purbeck – its name deriving from the old
English word 'corf' meaning 'a pass, or cutting'. The entire structure is
partially surrounded by a steep ditch. The largest man-made structure in
the region, this was a sight well known to Enid Blyton, visible as it was
from as far away as the town of Poole, even in its ruined state.

It would be futile to attempt to prove that 'Kirrin Castle' in 'The Famous
Five' books bears more than a passing resemblance to the real-life Corfe
Castle, when the former was clearly based on an image which Enid drew
from her subconscious. Nevertheless, the two do have some intriguing
features in common: a tumbledown gatehouse (in the case of Corfe there
are two); walls with 'slit-like windows'; a space (at Corfe more than one) at
the end of a room, 'where the fireplace must [once] have been.'[1] Of course,
jackdaws are plentiful at Corfe Castle, just as they were at Kirrin.

There are even occasions when Corfe Castle appears to be set on an island
(even though it is not.). This happens when atmospheric conditions result
in temperature inversion, causing mist to collect around the mound on
which Corfe Castle stands; a breathtaking phenomenon which is often to
be observed early on a crisp, bright, autumnal morning. However, whereas
the dungeons of 'Kirrin Castle' are situated underground, those of Corfe
Castle are not – or if so, they have yet to be discovered.

In her letter to *Teachers' World* in 1931, Enid expressed a desire to, 'see back
through a few hundred years and know exactly what the castle [Corfe] had
looked like…,' and she guessed correctly, that there had once been knights
here, that in days gone by it had been attacked by enemies, and that
gunpowder had been used to blow it up. However, when Corfe Castle was
blown up, this was only after its defenders had been betrayed from within,
as will shortly be demonstrated. In fact, the true story was one which

would have thrilled even such experienced adventure seekers as 'The Famous Five' themselves!

From the reign of King William I (1066-87) until that of Queen Elizabeth I, Corfe was a royal castle. After this time it passed into private ownership. Although the oldest parts of the castle date from Saxon times, it was under the Normans that it achieved its spectacular grandeur. In its final form, Corfe Castle consisted of three separately defensible areas or wards; the inner ward containing the mighty twelfth-century keep, built in the reign of Henry I. The entire structure is surrounded by towers, joined by an intervening curtain wall. Both the inner and outer gateways comprise two round towers with gateway arch and portcullis.

In its time, Corfe Castle has witnessed many of the important events of English history, including the assassination of King Edward (subsequently known as The Martyr) in 978. However, perhaps the castle's most celebrated incumbent was Lady Mary Bankes, under whose leadership it

 successfully withstood the siege of 1643 (during the Civil War), but failed to withstand a second siege in 1646, when its defenders were betrayed by treachery.[2] Following the fall of the castle, the House of Commons ordered it to be slighted (demolished by explosives), hence its present condition.

Lady Mary Bankes.
Photo: the National Trust.

In the 1920s and 1930s, Corfe Castle (part of the Bankes Estate – Lady Mary Bankes' property having been restored to her at the end of the Civil War) was opened to the public.

Eight
SWANAGE'S RAILWAY

In 'The Famous Five' story *Five go Adventuring Again* (published 1943), George (Georgina) and Anne travelled down together on the train from their boarding school to 'the little station that served Kirrin', to spend a holiday at Kirrin Cottage, the home of George's parents.

In those days, the train would have been powered by steam, in the same way as in the real-life scenario, as described by Gillian when, 'One day we [herself, her mother Enid, and her sister Imogen] took the train [from Swanage] to the little village of Corfe, with its narrow, twisting street of small, grey stone houses.'[1]

✧ ✧ ✧

The origin of the Swanage Railway was as follows. Although the London and South Western Railway's (LSWR) Southampton to Dorchester line was

opened on 1 June 1847, it was not until 20 May 1885 that the Wareham to Swanage branch line was created. It had picturesque stations, 24 cuttings, 23 embankments, seven iron girder bridges and several stone bridges, including a stone viaduct at Corfe Castle.[2]

At Corfe Castle Railway Station.

✧ ✧ ✧

A measure of just how dangerous a place Swanage was in the dark days of the war is illustrated by the experience of Peter Dyson, who as a boy lived in Wareham, and travelled to school in Swanage on the same train as was used by Enid and her children in March 1940, and doubtless on subsequent holidays. (The railways of Britain were controlled by the State for the duration of the Second World War.)

'In the early months of the Second World War,' said Peter, 'everything seemed to be much as before on the local railway scene.' However, 'strictly enforced lighting restrictions on trains and stations were an obvious difference, [the so-called blackout] and travelling at night by train became difficult and often unreliable. Station name-boards and other identifications were often removed to confuse possible enemy agents…. This period also brought train loads of evacuees to this part of Dorset from London.'[3]

On 3 February 1943, Peter and his fellow pupils were aboard the train, which was about to set off from Swanage on its return journey at the end of the school day when: '…suddenly there was a tremendous roar above the station and an aircraft swept very low above the train and platform. We looked out of the carriage windows and the driver, fireman, guard and signalman were running and shouting to us to get out of the train and [take shelter] under the carriages. Almost immediately the aircraft was upon us with a shattering roar of engine and machine-gun fire. The effect of the gunfire was to completely strip out the glass roof of the station and much damage was done to the carriage roofs and the station's superstructure. There were many casualties. The locomotive was damaged in the attack and the aircraft dropped a high-explosive bomb [as it over flew the station] which passed straight through the front of the nearby Railway Hotel, but fortunately did not explode.' [In Clifford. P.20.] On the same day there was bomb damage to cottages in Church Hill and the roof of Swanage's Parish Church of St Mary, with the destruction of 14 of its windows.

Nine
WAR – THE TIDE TURNS

Enid and Hugh's decree nisi was granted in December 1942. In January 1943, the first American forces began arriving in Britain; some of the service men and women being billeted in hotels and guest houses, and others with private families in Swanage. Meanwhile, the town raised the sum of £65,000 in that year's 'Wings for Victory' fundraising campaign in support of the Royal Air Force.

Enid and Kenneth Darrell Waters were married on 20 October 1943, at the City of Westminster Registry Office, and spent their honeymoon at St Ives, Cornwall. (Six days after Enid's wedding, her first husband Hugh, married Ida Crowe at the City of London Registry Office, the couple going on to have a daughter Rosemary.) By now Swanage had become a permanent part of Enid's life, and in the years that followed, she and Kenneth would stay at the town's Hotel Grosvenor two or three times a year, sometimes with the children and at other times without them.

For the next two decades, in addition to her other writings, Enid produced a 'Famous Five' book every year, many of which, to the discerning reader, contained tantalising glimpses of the Isle of Purbeck.

Swanage's Hotel Grosvenor had some important visitors on 17 April 1944, namely King George VI, Field Marshal Bernard Montgomery, General Sir Miles Dempsey and Field Marshal Lord Alanbrooke. Here, they dined and spent the night, before being taken to a concrete pillbox overlooking Studland Bay for the final dress rehearsal for the Normandy Invasion (codename 'Smash III'). This commenced before dawn the following morning, in the presence of British Prime Minister Winston Churchill and American President Dwight D. Eisenhower, who were assigned to a special bunker built by Canadian Army sappers and known as 'Fort Henry'.[1]

On the eve of D-Day, 6 June 1944, Swanage Bay was packed with troops, landing craft and escort vessels, and when hostilities commenced the following day, the fiery glow over the sky from the direction of Cherbourg was clearly visible from Swanage.[2]

For Enid, holidays in Swanage continued, notwithstanding the fact that the war in Europe had as yet almost another year to run. In the summer of 1944, Imogen said this involved:

> … driving down through The New Forest, where we stopped for a picnic and watched the ponies. The ferry across Poole Harbour was not yet open, so we drove via Wareham and Corfe Castle, which my mother used in later stories. The roads were almost empty and we began to invent games to play to pass the time. One point for an inn, two for a bicycle and so on. We competed for the first sight of the sea, which comes when you are quite close to the town [of Swanage] and drove to the western end where the Hotel Grosvenor [now demolished] perched above its own private beach. It was a large building, part white concrete and part orange-red brick and quite extraordinarily ugly.[3]

The steep hill that rose behind the hotel provided the view for Gillian and me that year. To the west was the precipitous and rocky coastline, along which houses are now landscaped, but which was then home only to the sea birds and further on a lighthouse. The front of the hotel, where in later years we shared a suite with my parents, looked over the sea, past the two piers, towards the Old Harry Rocks at the eastern end of the bay, with Bournemouth beyond; and to the south, on a clear day, The Needles [Isle of Wight]. The hotel had a revolving door into the hall and a slow lift to its several floors, as well as carpeted stairs and long corridors. It had a big restaurant on the ground floor with a ballroom above.

The swimming pool was empty and the private beach covered in tank-traps – rusty scaffolding erections that leaned out towards the sea. There were also mines. However, part of the town beach had been cleared and that is where we went as a family, to swim and play. I learnt to swim that summer, first with my rubber ring and then [took] the first few gulping strokes on my own. My step-father [Kenneth] swam quite well; a rather stiff and precise crawl. His small body, beautifully muscled, looked superb in bathing trunks and he and my mother must have made a handsome middle-aged couple. My mother wore a bathing costume with a decorous skirt. She swam wearing a bathing cap, a gentle breast stroke, and coming out of the water would remove her cap from her wiry, dark hair and sit beside my step-father with her legs tucked on one side....

Swanage I loved. The two piers, one old and wooden and rotting and the other a little newer and made of iron, curved out to sea together like good friends. Motor torpedo boats substituted for the paddle steamers that eventually returned to ferry passengers to and from Bournemouth. The Old Harry Rocks, with the sea washing round them were objects of wonder, and I loved the smell and the sound and the ever-changing sight of the sea. We stayed at Swanage for exactly two weeks and then packed our suitcases again and drove back home.[4]

✧ ✧ ✧

In this, and in the following two years, Enid was offered the presidency of the Swanage Regatta and Carnival Committee (devoted to supporting local charities), which she accepted.

An autographing session at Hill and Churchill's Bookshop. Photo: Gillian Baverstock.

Ten

THE HOTEL GROSVENOR

That Enid's holidays spent at the Hotel Grosvenor were for her, blissfully happy ones, is born out by cine film, showing a smiling Enid entertaining children on the terrace. Also, there were eyewitness accounts of her walking across the beach with the children, prior to going for a bathe, or embarking in one of the clinker-built rowing boats which were fashionable at the time.

✧ ✧ ✧

The hotel had started life as a private house known as The Grove, and was built by a Mr Coventry in 1838. His state-of-the-art marine residence included drawing room, dining room, library, conservatory, brew house and pleasure gardens. He also built a coach house, and cottages to house the coachman and gardener,[1] and laid out, 'new roads, terraces and gardens....'[2]

The Hotel Grosvenor.　　Photo: Dennis Smale.

In 1866 (following the death of Coventry's widow), The Grove was purchased by Thomas Docwra, a retired civil engineer from London. In 1890, The Grove passed into the hands of the Williams family, who subsequently enlarged it and converted it into an hotel. In the early-twentieth century, the hotel (which incidentally also owned the pier) was purchased by the Exton family, who enlarged it even further, and renamed it the Hotel Grosvenor.

✧ ✧ ✧

In Enid's time, the hotel was furnished and decorated in the art nouveau style, with a dining room which could seat 300 guests, and a ballroom with sprung floor and resident band.[3] Favourite dances at that time were the 'Snowball' and the 'Hokey-Cokey'.[4] Imogen, it has to be said, did not like the Hotel Grosvenor. She found it, 'large, ugly and pretentious and many of its guests seemed to me to share these characteristics.'

The Second World War finally ended in Europe on 8 May 1945, and in the Far East on 14 August 1945. To celebrate, a victory dance was held at the Hotel Grosvenor in aid of Swanage Hospital.[5]

Eleven
SHIPWRECK ON 'KIRRIN ISLAND': A REAL-LIFE SHIPWRECK: SWANAGE'S FIRST LIFEBOAT

From her vantage point at the Hotel Grosvenor, Enid would have looked out across the broad sweep of Swanage Bay in all its moods, towards Ballard Down, with its 300-foot-high cliffs, and the Old Harry Rocks (named after a Poole pirate Harry Paye). She would have seen Swanage's fleet of fishing boats, which were vital in those days to the economy of the town, and which were obliged to take shelter to avoid the easterly gales to which Swanage was so exposed. At low tide, she could not have failed to notice the sinister rocky ledges, protruding like fingers into the sea; there to trap any unsuspecting mariner unfamiliar with that particular stretch of coastline. Finding herself in surroundings such as these, the attraction of writing a story about a shipwreck would surely prove to be irresistible!

Sure enough, in Enid's first 'Famous Five' book, *Five on a Treasure Island*, the children become excited when George informs them that on the far side of 'Kirrin Island' (which she happens to own) is the wreck of a ship; one of many whose masts are visible at low tide. George believes that this ship once belonged to a great-great-great grandfather of hers, and that it was carrying a cargo of 'big bars of gold'[1] (which modern-day divers had subsequently been unable to locate).

They row out to the wreck, determining its position by taking bearings from a church tower, from a hilltop on the mainland, and from the two towers of 'Kirrin Castle' on the island. On their next excursion, they plan to stay longer, so they take with them a picnic of sandwiches, ripe plums and ginger pop. When a storm breaks, they are amazed as the force of the waves lifts the wreck up and deposits it, 'on to the sharp teeth of the dangerous rocks on the south west side....'[2]

On their next visit they tie their boat up to the wreck itself, and then climb on to it, but find nothing unusual, until Julian notices a small cupboard in the wall of the captain's cabin. George produces a pocket knife to force the door open and inside they find and recover a wooden box stamped with the initials HJK – the name of George's great-great-great grandfather Henry John Kirrin, the captain and owner of the ship.

There is a minor panic when, on their return, Uncle Quentin confiscates the wooden box, but Julian saves the day by retrieving it while he (Quentin) is having his afternoon nap. Having forced open the box, inside it they find a diary of the ship's voyages, and also a map of 'Kirrin Castle' in the days before it was a ruin. The word 'ingots' printed in 'old-fashioned letters' on the map, indicates that the castle is the hiding place for the gold. Julian duly takes a copy of the map and replaces the box, before Uncle Quentin notices its absence.

Tension builds when Uncle Quentin sells the box to an antique dealer, which makes the children fear that the hiding place of the gold may now no longer be a secret. However, the story ends happily, with 'The Famous Five' getting the better of the three villains who are attempting to steal the gold.

(In *Five have a Mystery to Solve*, the elements come into play once again when the children's boat is swept up onto the shore of 'Whispering Island' by powerful tides.)

The coast of Purbeck was, and still remains particularly dangerous for shipping. In Purbeck, a particular danger derives from ledges, projections of rock stretching out into the sea and invisible, especially at high tide. The Peveril Ledge, for example, at Peveril Point, is but a few minutes walk from the Hotel Grosvenor. Local builder and historian William Masters Hardy (1836-1921), writing in 1910, recalled that: 'Within the past sixty years [i.e. 1850-1910] there have, to my knowledge, been twelve or fourteen ships wrecked on the ledges off Peveril Point and elsewhere.'[3]

Enid was an ardent supporter of Swanage's lifeboat, whose lifeboat house and slipway (built in 1875) was situated adjacent to the Hotel Grosvenor, between it and Peveril Point. Gillian clearly remembers – during her holidays with her mother in Swanage – watching the lifeboat being launched and performing its practice manoeuvres. (The lifeboats at that time were the *Thomas Markby* 1928-49 and the *R.L.P.* 1949-75, which saved a total of 27 and, amazingly, 240 lives respectively, during their times in service.)

It was in fact as a result of a terrifying shipwreck that occurred on the Peveril Ledge on 21 January 1875 that Swanage acquired its first lifeboat. The vessel involved was the *Wild Wave*, a 134-ton brigantine, en route from Newcastle-upon-Tyne to Poole with a cargo of coal, which for some unexplained reason, overshot the entrance to Poole Harbour and continued on westwards. This is the official RNLI account of what followed:

At 4.30 a.m., dead low water, the *Wild Wave* was making for Poole with a fair, southerly breeze, when she suddenly struck with great violence on jagged rocks off Peveril Point. Although there was a thick haze, the coastguard saw the accident, ordered two gigs to be manned, and the rocket apparatus taken to the cliffs. [A reference to the Dennett's rocket apparatus, invented and patented by John Dennett 1780-1852, of New Village, Isle of Wight, which enabled the rescuer to fire a rope-line at a stricken ship, thereby providing a means for its occupants to escape.]

The second [rocket] line fired fell between the masts and was secured, but no sooner had this been done than the vessel fell over on her beam ends, breaking the rocket line. Another line was fired across the wreck, but there was now no sign of life, although a steam tug and the Branksea [Brownsea] lifeboat, which managed to reach the vessel, found her crew still aboard and alive. Some time later the Poole lifeboat came into the bay under oars and sail, by which time nothing of the brigantine was left, other than a few broken spars.[4]

The event was witnessed by the influential Sir Charles Robinson (advisor in art to the South Kensington – later Victoria and Albert – Museum), a resident of Swanage, who was so impressed with the bravery of the coastguard Mr John Lose and his officers, that he wrote to *The Times* newspaper declar-

Launch of Swanage's second lifeboat, the William Erle, 28 December 1890.

Photo: David Haysom Collection.

ing that, in his opinion, Swanage was in need of a lifeboat. A Mr S.J. Wilde of London happened to see the letter, and he responded by donating £500 from the estate of his late aunt, Mrs Margaret Ryder Wilde, towards the purchase of Swanage's first lifeboat, the *Charlotte Mary*, a 'pulling' boat with ten oarsmen, which was launched from the boathouse, situated near Peveril Point, on 16 September 1875.

Enid's support for the lifeboat is reflected in two letters which she wrote (in immaculate longhand) to RNLI Secretary Colonel A.D. Burnett Brown. In the first, sent from her home, Green Hedges, and dated 20 June 1952, she informs Colonel Brown that she hopes, 'soon to be in a position to recommend various excellent charities and missions and [good] works for children,' saying that, 'the Lifeboat Service is so good for the boys in particular. I am just off to Swanage,' she says, 'and shall probably see our valiant lifeboat there in action – always a tremendous excitement.' In the second letter, sent four days later from Swanage's Hotel Grosvenor, Enid refers to a proposed essay competition on the subject of the history of the lifeboat service, of which she is strongly in favour, to be promoted by the RNLI for elementary schools:[5]

'If ever you would like to use the pulling power of my name as far as children are concerned, you have only to ask me.' She offers to write up, 'one of your true and really wonderful stories,' [i.e. of real-life lifeboat rescues] which:

> …would be a real labour of love, to bring the ideas and ideals of the lifeboat service right into the hearts of all the children who already know my books so well. I am not merely a storyteller, but [I] do try to inculcate the right ideas into children's minds, and to tell them about such fine institutions as yours,

the PDSA [People's Dispensary for Sick Animals], St John's Ambulance Cadets, and all the rest....

Finally, she points out how, in her view: 'The honour and privilege of serving others has fallen out of fashion for too long, especially where children are concerned. I take every chance I can of bringing it back!'

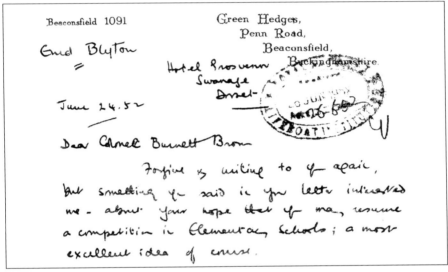

Letter from Enid to RNLI.   Photo: RNLI, Poole.

(Incidentally, this letter leaves the recipient in no doubt as to Enid's eloquence, and masterful use of syntax and vocabulary.)

Twelve
FIVE GO TO SMUGGLERS' TOP

Five go to Smugglers' Top (published 1945) begins at 'Kirrin Cottage', with mention of 'Kirrin Island' and 'Kirrin Station'. However, on this occasion the children are unable to stay with their cousin Georgina (George) at 'Kirrin Cottage', owing to damage caused by a tree falling on to the building in a storm. Instead, 'The Five' (including George and her dog Timmy) go to stay with a friend of George's father (Uncle Quentin) named Mr Lenoir; he is the stepfather of Pierre, known as 'Sooty' (who is in the same class as Dick at school).

This was the fourth book in the series, and by now the characters of 'The Famous Five' are becoming apparent to the readers. Julian, a natural leader, is a foil to his sometimes over-exuberant younger colleagues. Dick, who has a keen sense of humour, is not averse to facing danger, and performs such exploits as shinning up and down the ropes of water wells, should the need arise. George (Georgina), who is self-confident, brave, loyal and absolutely truthful, has a temper which can sometimes get the better of her. Her ability in swimming, boat-handling and rock climbing is much admired by the boys. [In fact, says Gillian, Enid once told her agent that she realized that George in 'The Famous Five' was a reflection of herself as a child.'[1]] Anne is gentle, kind and friendly, but fearful of adventures and frightened of the dark. She is also imaginative (which George is not). Anne matures into a confident and sensible young lady. Finally, Timmy comes in useful as guard

Enid reading stories to children in garden of Green Hedges.
Photo: National Magazine Co., London.

dog, explorer of caves and tunnels, pursuer of villains, and of course is a good companion. As for their parents, the children perceive them as a necessary encumbrance, who, fortunately for them, are invariably summoned away at the beginning of the school holiday on urgent business, only to return at the end to hear all about the children's adventures!

Sooty's house, 'Smugglers' Top', situated on 'Castaway Hill', is described as 'very old' and, 'built on the top of a strange hill surrounded by marshes over which the sea once flowed.... Smuggling went on there in the old days.' The children are warned not to go walking on the marsh, which would suck them down in no time if they set foot on it. The house has a single tower, and Sooty tells them that he has seen light shining from it, 'on certain nights.'[2] Also, he says that lower down the hill lives a man called Barling, who is a rich and powerful smuggler!

Sooty shows 'The Five' a secret passage, leading from the hallway of 'Smugglers' Top' into the cupboard in his bedroom. There is also another passage which runs from Sooty's bedroom, 'out by a secret tunnel that opens half way down the town....' This is part of a large system of catacombs which are situated deep down in the bowels of the hill. The children explore the tunnel at the end of which they find themselves, 'somewhere on the steep cliff side that ran down to the marsh.'[3]

One night the children realize that someone is signalling from the tower room and that, 'the line of tiny, pricking lights...' which they can see is in fact, 'smugglers – coming over a secret path from the sea to Castaway Hill!' Mr Lenoir has a manservant named Block, who affects to be deaf. The children's suspicions about Block prove to be well-founded, when they discover that it was he who has been signalling from the tower. The tension mounts as George's father Uncle Quentin, comes to stay and is kidnapped by Barling and taken down into the tunnels. Barling confesses that he is a smuggler. 'I make a lot of money from it,' he says. 'It is easy to run a smuggling trade here, because no one can control the marshes, or stop men using the secret path that only I and a few others know.'[4] It transpires that the reason Barling has kidnapped Uncle Quentin is because the latter has produced plans for the draining of the marshes, which would mean the end of the former's smuggling activities.

Finally, with the aid of Timmy (who performs some heroic antics, such as tackling Block and Barling, and helping to locate the children when they become lost in the catacombs and shepherding them to the waiting police), Uncle Quentin is rescued and all is well.

As a frequent visitor to Purbeck, Enid was undoubtedly aware of the extent of the vast systems of subterranean tunnels in the vicinity of Swanage, the result of centuries of stone mining in the region. These tunnels, which were also reputed to be linked to certain properties, private, manorial and ecclesiastical, were said once to have been the haunt of smugglers. It was even suggested (fancifully) that smuggled goods landed at the Tilly Whim cliffside quarry, were transported by underground tunnel to Corfe Castle, four miles away!

For once in a 'Famous Five' story, however, Enid's sub-conscious mind may have thrown up a feature that does not exist in Dorset, namely 'Castaway Hill', which is more reminiscent of St Michael's Mount, situated at Mount's Bay, near Penzance, which Enid may first have seen in 1943, whilst on her honeymoon at St Ives in Cornwall with her second husband Kenneth.

However, an even more likely contender for the inspiration for Castaway Hill is one indicated by John Rowley of the Purbeck Mineral and Mining Museum. Says he, several people who have visited the museum:

> …tell me that as teenagers, they used to go into the clay mines at the bottom of Creech Barrow and come out at the top, and that it was just as Enid described it. At the time of her writing the book, it would have been possible for Enid to do the same. However, the top of Creech Barrow has subsided approximately 6 metres, so today this feat would be impossible.

It should be mentioned that Creech Barrow is a prehistoric burial mound, situated atop Creech Barrow Hill, 2½ miles west of Corfe Castle.

Thirteen
SMUGGLING IN PURBECK

Enid was a sociable person, and from such people as the local Swanage fishermen, who frequented the sea shore and piers in the vicinity of the Hotel Grosvenor, she would have heard true stories of smuggling carried out in Purbeck in former times. Because of its relative remoteness, this was an ideal location for smugglers, who made good use of the natural coastal caves and the cliffside quarries with their deep tunnels. It therefore comes as little surprise to find that smuggling tales feature strongly in many of Enid's books.

Coastguard station, Peveril Point, circa 1905.
Photo: David Haysom Collection.

One of the most fascinating of all local smugglers in times gone by was Charles Hayward, born in the village of Langton Matravers (two miles to the west of Swanage) in 1796, and outwardly a respectable pillar of the community.

Following in the footsteps of his forebears, Charles became a quarryman, and subsequently rented the nearby Dancing Ledge cliff-side quarry. In 1846 he was appointed Langton's Parish Clerk, and in 1860 he became the village's first regular sub-postmaster, the Post Office being situated at Fig Tree Cottage in the High Street (which was also his home.)[1]

Fortunately for posterity, Charles' grandson, William Charles Talbot Dean (born 1859), kept a diary which clearly implicates his grandfather in smuggling, the entry for 23 October 1869 reading as follows:

> Today happened great adventures with grandfather [i.e. Charles Hayward]. Last evening he asked me if I felt well

Charles Hayward, church warden and smuggler!

Photo: Langton Matravers Local History and Preservation Society.

enough to assist him in some business matter.... This evening, just after dusk I was requested by my grandfather to stand outside the church gate – but not to look too involved with anything in particular – and so I must needs walk to and fro past the gate, and not stand too still.... My grandfather also gave me strict instructions to alert him – he being within the church – if a peeler [policeman] – came up or down the road. Seven gentlemen came variously to meet my grandfather, and they all went inside the church. A peeler came down from Garfield, past me and thence [went] on to Steppes [the next hamlet.]

I had given the alert: taking my cap off, shaking it and putting it on again, and whilst the peeler walked bye (sic) all was silent in the church, nor any lights. Presently came two stone carts... and the seven gentlemen came out and assisted the drivers with unloading the stone; these were stacked flat-down and not up-down. The men then brought in barrels of all sizes and different shapes. Altogether this went into the church – I could not see where, but I heard a bell make a half-sounding, and heard a man say something bad. They then I think, came to the porch, and the two drivers took papers from my grandfather and reloaded the stone and drove off to Steppes. I heard much talking; my grandfather came out to me, thanked me profusely for my assistance, and gave me a gold coin. I went home and straight to bed.[2]

In 1872, Charles was appointed Rector's Warden at Langton's Parish Church of St George (the one referred to in W.C.T. Dean's diary.) When in 1874, Langton's rector, the Reverend E.F. Trotman, deemed the nave of the church to be in a deplorable condition, even though it had been rebuilt only as recently as forty-five years previously, historian R.J. Saville (writing in 2001) is certain where the blame lay: 'There can be little doubt,' he wrote, 'that the activities of Charles Hayward and his companions were a contributory factor to the short life of Langton's middle [i.e. rebuilt] church.'³ In other words, by storing their barrels of contraband in the church roof, the smugglers had caused such damage that the entire nave of the church had to be demolished and rebuilt. As for Hayward, who apparently led a charmed life, he was never apprehended for his smuggling activities, and died in 1879 at the age of eighty-two.

At Dancing Ledge, where Charles Hayward rented a quarry from the Serrell family of Durnford House, Langton, there exists a swimming pool, man-made after Charles's time (about which more will be said later). It is therefore interesting to note that in her book, *First Term at Malory Towers* (published 1946), there is mention of a similar outdoor swimming pool set on the coast and hewn out of solid rock.

Fourteen
HOLIDAYS IN POST-WAR SWANAGE

With the coming of the end of the war, Enid and her family's holidays in Swanage continued, albeit in an altogether more peaceful atmosphere. 'Holidays are jumbled up in memory,' said Gillian. 'Riding on the downs [Enid did not ride]; fishing for mackerel with hooks baited with bicycle valves; learning to sail a 15 feet dinghy; diving through waves in a storm-tossed sea; walking across the springy downland on Purbeck hills with my mother, where the larks sang and a multitude of flowers bloomed.' For her this represented, 'two weeks of magic that fade away with your suntan – but there's always next year!'[1]

Husband Kenneth encouraged Enid to play golf, first at Wentworth, Surrey, and later at the Isle of Purbeck Golf Club.[2]

Gillian and Imogen in Swanage near slipway at end of The Parade. Photo: Gillian Baverstock.

'In the evenings she enjoyed whatever was going on in the hotel: there were dances twice a week, a bridge drive once a week, billiards and ping-pong tournaments, beetle drives, quizzes, etc....[3] They occasionally went to the theatre,' said Gillian, 'but because Kenneth had had his hearing damaged at the Battle of Jutland and was deaf, musicals were really all that he could enjoy.'[4]

According to younger daughter Imogen, Enid 'took *The Daily Telegraph* [newspaper,] and for many years did the crossword in the evenings, often completing it and sending off the prize one at weekends'. She also practised embroidery, and for years, 'mended the family's clothes, with beautiful darns and tiny stitches. This was an evening occupation, when her work was put away.'[5] However, in holiday time, such tasks were held in abeyance. 'My stepfather was very adamant that it should be a restful and relaxing time for her,' said Gillian, 'because she worked so hard [during] the rest of her life.'[6] As for her writing:

From the beginning she [Enid] wrote to a routine. In the [19]20s and [19]30s, she usually wrote only in the mornings. However, as her work increased in the [19]40s and [19]50s she worked all day when she was writing a novel, although she took time off to visit London, or to play golf. She never worked at weekends, and as little as possible on holiday. Every day, she had to find time to correct proofs, check art work and answer her many letters.[7]

Throughout the [19]40s and [19]50s Enid wrote 13 series of books for older children: adventure stories, school stories, mystery stories, magical stories, circus stories and farming stories. There were at least 13 other series for younger children: ranging from comic strip books (*Mary Mouse*), through story collections (*Amelia Jane*), to '*Noddy*' and '*Bom*'. She also published a number of stand-alone books like *The Boy Next Door*, or *Smuggler Ben*.'[8] Enid's prodigious speed of writing enabled her to produce a 'Noddy' book in two days, and an 'adventure' book in five and a half days. However, she [Enid] did not write much when she was away.... I never saw her bring her typewriter [a portable Imperial] with her.

Nevertheless, Enid did, when on holiday, attend book signings (at Hill and Churchill's bookshop in Swanage) with Gillian, whose job it was to blot the books as she signed them, 'because of course, we used ink [fountain] pens in those days, and it would have been awful if it [the book] was shut and it was smudged, because the child would have been devastated.' A youthful admirer of Enid was Susan Prust from Wimborne, whose father ran regular film shows at the Hotel Grosvenor. He also took an 8mm film of Enid, Susan, and Susan's toy rabbit 'Wilfred Pickles' (which she had won in a competition at the hotel), sitting on the terrace.

Astonishingly by modern standards, Enid was able to take her holidays in Swanage entirely undisturbed by the media. For example, George Willey, who has written a column in *The Swanage Advertiser* for the past fifty years, never in all that time wrote a story about Enid. 'Today a celebrated author, and even the most minor figures, are besieged with all kinds of attention,' he said, but 'in those days Enid Blyton was permitted to lead an absolutely normal life, and [to] take her children down to the water's edge and nobody would actually stop and talk to her, or dream of accosting her and saying, "Aren't you the famous Enid Blyton?"'[9]

Enid, 'swam most days [and played a good game of tennis]. She and my stepfather used to swim round the pier and then round both piers. I remember my pride when I achieved each distance!' said Gillian. This was no mean feat, when there was water traffic in the shape of fishing boats and paddle steamers, besides wind and tide to contend with!

The precedent for sea bathing off England's southern coast was set in 1789 by King George III who, with his wife Queen Charlotte and the three princesses, paid a visit to Weymouth. Here, the King allegedly became the first English monarch to avail himself of the use of a bathing machine. This was a covered carriage with large wheels, designed to be pulled into the sea, its function being to allow bathers to change into their swimming attire and enter the water discreetly, without causing offence to passers by. From then on, sea bathing became increasingly popular.

Local historian William Masters Hardy recalled the time when, at first, there was only a single bathing machine on Swanage beach. 'If anyone wanted to bathe from it, a day's notice had to be given to the proprietor at The Anchor Inn, who would provide the services of a horse, man, and nurse, as the machine was never allowed to be used without the proper attendants being present.'[10] However, so popular did the pastime of sea bathing become in Swanage that by 1910, 'we now see between 200 and 300 of all shapes and makes, from the old-fashioned wooden bathing machines to the latest hygienic tents, as well as many coloured and prettily designed private tents.'[11]

Edwardian Swanage – seafront with bathing machine. Photo: David Haysom Collection.

Fifteen

FIRST TERM AT MALORY TOWERS: DANCING LEDGE: DURNFORD SCHOOL: LULWORTH CASTLE

Enid's *First Term at Malory Towers,* published in 1946 and the first in a series of six books, was about the life of a school of that name; Darrell Rivers being the heroine of the story, and Alicia Johns, her classmate. (Enid, with her impish sense of humour, chose Darrell which was her husband's middle name, and Rivers which was akin to Waters, his surname.)

To quote from the story:

> They rounded a corner, Alicia nudged her [Darrell's] arm. 'There you are, look! Over there, on that hill! The sea is behind, far down the cliff, but you can't see that, of course.' Darrell looked. She saw a big, square building of soft, grey stone standing high upon a hill. The hill was really a cliff, that fell steeply down to the sea. At each end of the gracious building stood rounded towers. Darrell could glimpse two other towers behind as well, making four in all. North tower, south, east and west.

As for the school:

> One of the things that Darrell liked best of all [about it] was the big swimming pool down by the sea. This had been hollowed out of a stretch of rocks, so that it had a nice, rocky, uneven bottom. Seaweed grew at the sides, and sometimes the rocky bed of the pool felt a little slimy. But the sea swept into the big, natural pool each day, filled it, and made lovely waves all across it.[1]

Is it possible, from the description of the school building in *Last Term at Malory Towers* (published 1950), that it was Dorset's Lulworth Castle (situated 4 miles south-west of Wareham, and about 2 miles from Lulworth Cove) that Enid had in mind? (This, despite the fact that there is mention of the 'dark-blue Cornish sea' beyond the school.)[2] The similarity between the two is striking, both being squarely built with a round tower at each corner.

It also seems more than likely that the seaside swimming pool described in 'Malory Towers' was based on the (previously described) real-life, artificially constructed pool at Dancing Ledge.

The story of how this pool came to be built is as follows: the village of Langton Matravers once boasted six schools, of which the Durnford Preparatory School for Boys was one. Durnford was established in 1893 by Thomas Pellatt MA, at Durnford House in Langton's High Street. This was the building that had once belonged to the Serrell family, from whom the smuggler Charles Hayward rented the Dancing Ledge cliff-side quarry, as already mentioned. Pellatt was a kindly man, who believed in fresh air and freedom for his boys.

It was a tradition for Durnford's schoolboys to commence their day with a brisk walk down the steep path to Dancing Ledge (which was also owned by the school), where they swam naked in the sea (Durnford having no swimming pool of its own). However, there were dangers attendant in this, an intimation of which was given by surgeon and historian Sir Frederick Treves, who wrote in 1906:

> In the place of the beach [i.e where one might expect to find a beach], a flat, acre-wide slab of rock slides into the sea… the sea swirls smoothly over the glacis, as [if] it were feeling it with blind hands, and then falls off by the far end into a pool of foam. An iron ladder leads down to the Ledge, which is a place slippery with death in a rising tide.[3]

The prudent Pellatt therefore, fearing an accident, had an artificial swimming pool created here, using explosives to blast a large cavity out of the rocky ledge.

Sixteen

FIVE ON KIRRIN ISLAND AGAIN:
QUARRIES: MINES: SECRET PASSAGES

Five on Kirrin Island Again was published in 1947, by which time Enid's books had made their appearance in all the English-speaking countries, and The Boys' Club of America had awarded *The Island of Adventure* the prize for being the best junior book.

Enid and her books.
Photo: *Good Housekeeping.*

In addition to 'Kirrin Island' and 'Kirrin Castle' with its customary dungeons and jackdaws, the story features quarries, secret underground tunnels and a lighthouse-like tower. The children visit George (Georgina) and duly arrive at 'Kirrin', having travelled by train, to be met at the station by Aunt Fanny with the pony and trap. George announces that her father intends to go and live on 'Kirrin Island' which she owns, 'to do some special work' which involves building, 'a sort of tower or something in the castle yard.' En route to 'Kirrin Cottage' they see 'Kirrin Island', where 'a tall, thin tower, rather like a lighthouse' is situated at the top of which was, 'a glass-enclosed room, which glistened in the sun.'[1]

Having rowed their boat to 'Kirrin Island', they find the castle, which has two towers, one of which is almost a complete ruin. The other is inhabited by George's father Uncle Quentin. However, having failed to discover Uncle Quentin's whereabouts, they decide to explore a cave, the only one on the island which is accessible, either from the seaward side via a tunnel which runs beneath a shelf of rock, or by, 'dropping down a rope through a hole in the roof....'[2] Quentin suddenly appears, saying that he has been in his work-room, but he does not reveal to the children where this workroom is situated. As the children leave the island they notice 'a cloud of jackdaws' rising up into the air, and cawing loudly, as if they had been disturbed.

On a visit to a nearby quarry, they find a passage, discovered by Timmy the dog as he is digging for a rabbit, and decide that it is, 'just an old tunnel made by the quarrymen.' They befriend Martin, whose father Mr Curton possesses a magnificent radio, suitable for both transmitting and for receiving messages. Mr Curton tells the children that he is a journalist by profession.

The routine is that at 10.30 every morning, Uncle Quentin signals to them, by shining a light from the glass top of the tower - making six flashes to indicate that he is alright. This performance is repeated at 10.30 in the evening. One morning however, a total of 18 flashes come from the tower, which make the children wonder if Uncle Quentin is in some kind of danger. When they visit him to replenish his food supplies, he tells them that he has a feeling that, 'there's someone else on this island besides myself!'[3] George (reluctantly) leaves Timmy behind to be a guard dog for her father.

The local fishermen have been instructed by Uncle Quentin to keep visitors off the island, which makes Julian wonder if someone may have been landed there by parachute from an aeroplane. Using an old map of 'Kirrin Castle', which they found on a previous occasion, they discover that there are, in fact, two entrances to the castle's dungeons. 'The Famous Five' become angry when Martin, in whom they have confided, tells them that he has told his father Mr Curton, the secret of the tunnel beneath the shelf of rocks.

One night, George decides to visit 'Kirrin Island'. She is worried, because when her father signalled that morning in the customary way, Timmy was not with him in the tower, as was usually the case. She discovers a second tunnel, which she believes may lead her to the dungeons. Instead, it takes her down towards the sea. Suddenly, she finds herself in an enormous cave full of, 'wires, glass boxes' and, 'little machines that seem to be at work without a sound, whose centres were alive with funny, gleaming, shivering light.' [P.182.] She then realizes that she must be under the rocky bed of 'Kirrin Bay'.

Then she notices her father, sitting dejectedly at a table. He tells her that, 'Yes, two men were parachuted down on to the island, hoping to try and find out my secret,' which is the discovery of, 'a way of replacing all coal, coke and oil – an idea to give the world all the heat and power it wants, and to do away with mines and miners.'[4] Uncle Quentin entrusts his notebook containing the secret of his discoveries to George, who is captured by the men, but not before she has given the book to Timmy. He takes it in his mouth, and finds his way back to 'Kirrin Cottage' through the tunnel which leads to the quarry.

The story ends happily, with the arrest of the villains, and also of Mr Curton, who is in league with them. It also transpires that Mr Curton was Martin's guardian, not his father. The children agree that he (Martin), 'can come and play with us and go to the island, and Uncle Quentin will see if he can get you into an art school;'[5] this having been Martin's longstanding ambition.

The theme of signalling from towers is common to several of 'The Famous Five' stories, and in this, Enid's sub-conscious mind may have been drawing on such a feature in Purbeck, namely the lighthouse at Anvil Point, Durlston. Gillian recalls visiting it by day, and by night, its eerie lighting up of the sky would have been visible from Swanage. 'The Needles' lighthouse, situated at the westernmost point of the Isle of Wight, was also visible from Swanage's sea front on a clear day (albeit with the aid of binoculars).

Seventeen

PURBECK STONE

In *Five on Kirrin Island Again*, the phrase, 'At the bottom of the steps the tunnel seemed to be cut out of solid rock'[1] is strongly reminiscent of the stairway made in just such a way that leads from the cliffs at Durlston, on the south side of Swanage, down to the Tilly Whim cliff-side quarry. One may imagine Enid, having descended this stairway (which was in her time open to the public), staring into the unfathomable darkness of the huge man-made caves, and thinking to herself, how can I make this the background to a story?

The area of Purbeck, south of Swanage, and as far as Herston and beyond, was dotted in former times with numerous open-cast and subterranean stone mines, locally referred to as 'quarries', each rented from a landowner and worked by a family of the town; the first being dug in about 1650. Traditional attire for the quarrymen was moleskin waistcoats and trousers (made not from the skins of moles but from a coarse, twilled, cotton fabric called fustian), boots, cotton shirts and bowler hats. Men and boys, some only ten years old, worked by the dim light of a tallow candle (which they stuck either to the brim of their hat, or to the wall) in the damp, narrow, underground lanes, using only primitive hand tools to extract the stone.

Tilly Whim – a former cliff quarry.

At the cliff quarries, such as Dancing Ledge, Tilly Whim, Hedbury, Seacombe and Winspit, stone was obtained in a different way. A ledge was created halfway down the cliff, from which it was possible to burrow inwards, pillars being left in situ to support the roof.

The idyllic landscape of Purbeck, however, concealed a grim reality, particularly where children were concerned, for the truth was that in former times, those who worked with stone, particularly underground, were extremely vulnerable to accidental death or mutilation. Responding to reports of the deaths suffered by children in the mines, an elderly quarryman is reported to have told Swanage historian John T. Dean, 'They [the children] wuss cheap, plenty of 'em and more wur they come vrom.'[2] So had 'The Famous Five' been born to a local quarrying family of the time, their lives would have been very different indeed!

By the time Enid and her family came to Swanage for their holidays, virtually all remnants of the Swanage stone industry had disappeared except for

the tramway (linking the 'bankers' – repositories on the sea front where the stone blocks were stored – to the pier), parts of the rails of which exist even to this day, and also the weighbridge, where the stone was weighed. According to local historian W.M. Hardy however, 100 years previously these bankers contained stone:

Bankers of stone awaiting shipment.
Photo: David Haysom Collection.

… amounting to thousands of tonnes, stacked ready for shipment; while in the narrow streets and roads to the quarries would be seen a continuous line of [horse-drawn] stone wagons and carts, either returning empty or bringing fresh supplies of stone from the seemingly inexhaustible quarries.

From the bankers the stone was reloaded into horse-drawn carts and taken into the sea to be manually transferred into large, open boats (lighters), which took it out to the waiting ships which lay at anchor in the bay.

Such was the dexterity of the quarrymen, bankermen, loaders and sailors, that although some of the immense stones weighed sometimes 5 to 10 hundredweight, yet those shipping them had the knack of handling them like feathers, caps, or buttons....

In 1859, Swanage's first pier was constructed, and a tramway (with weighbridge) was laid down in order that horse-drawn trucks could convey the stone to it from the bankers, to be loaded directly onto the waiting ships, so that, 'In the days of its prosperity... Swanage... could boast a fleet of from 60 to 80 vessels.'[3]

Stone loading in Swanage Bay.
Photo: David Haysom Collection.

Eighteen
THE WELLINGTON CLOCK TOWER:
JOHN MOWLEM AND GEORGE BURT

As she walked along the shoreline from the Hotel Grosvenor towards the lifeboat station in the direction of Peveril Point, Enid would have noticed an impressive piece of architecture, situated in the very grounds of the hotel itself. The Wellington Clock Tower, built in memory of the Duke of Wellington, was originally situated at the approach to London Bridge. However, having been deemed to be an obstruction, it was removed in 1863, when it came into the possession of building contractor John Mowlem, a native of Swanage. In fact, according to W.M. Hardy, Mowlem, together with his father and three brothers, 'were the last gang of quarry-men who worked at Tilly Whim [cliff-side quarry].'

In 1867, Mowlem brought the clock tower to his home town of Swanage, and presented it to his friend and fellow London contractor, Thomas Docwra (mentioned previously), owner of The Grove (later the Hotel Grosvenor) since 1866, who re-erected it in what was then his garden. However, the original illuminated clock, which was displayed at the Great Exhibition at the Crystal Palace in 1851, was missing – its whereabouts being unknown.

The Wellington Clock Tower.

In fact Mowlem (and his wife's nephew George Burt, a partner in Mowlem's firm) brought to Swanage from London such a profusion of arte-facts (gleaned when they were engaged in restora-tion work in the city), that local historian David Lewer in 1971 amusingly described the town as 'Old London by the Sea'! They included Swanage

Town Hall's magnificent façade, which had originally belonged to the seventeenth-century Mercers Hall at Cheapside. Also numerous iron bollards, embossed with such logos as 'St Ann's, Soho' or 'St Martin's-in-the-Fields' which indicated their places of origin, were brought down from the capital to fulfil a similar function in Swanage.

On the site of the former stone bankers, Mowlem built an Institute, to include museum, reading room and library, which he presented to the town in 1863. It was also to be used 'for meetings and entertainment.'[1] To Enid, the Institute, and a nearby column erected by Mowlem to commemorate King Alfred's victory over the Danish fleet off Peveril Point in 877, would have been familiar sights. He also placed another monument at Court Hill, near the cottage where he was born, to honour the memory of the late Albert, Prince Consort.

George Burt, in 1862, purchased and laid out the 80-acre Durlston Park Estate, which included: shops, houses, promenades, and a 'castle' which he built at Durlston Head. Stone tablets were placed at intervals, inscribed with uplifting poetry and quotations from the Psalms, and also with geophysical and astronomical data. In 1887, Burt opened the Tilly Whim caves (which were part of the Estate) to the public as a tourist attraction; providing access by blasting out a tunnel through the rock, as already mentioned.

Nineteen

FAMILY FORTUNES

By 1947, said Imogen, 'Enid had become a very wealthy woman. Not only that, my stepfather [Kenneth] had acquired a taste for spending money.' Whereas Imogen's father Hugh had possessed a relatively modest black Rover motor car, 'with a rabbit mascot on the front', now Kenneth, 'bought a Rolls Royce for himself, and for a brief period had a Bentley as well. He bought a beautiful MG saloon for my mother and employed a

chauffeur to drive her, as well as to help in the garden.' Kenneth also 'invested heavily in his wine cellar…, which included clarets such as Chateau Latour and Chateau Lafite. In good time for the 1948 Olympic Games [held in London], a black and white television set in an enormous mahogany cabinet, was placed in the study….' However, Enid, 'did not like television at all. I suspect it was too pedestrian for her quick mind.' Enid for her part was, 'careful about how much [money] she spent.'[1]

Enid and Kenneth in garden with Bimbo the cat. Photo: *Daily Graphic.*

The Autumn of 1948 found the family once more at Swanage's Hotel Grosvenor, where the children, 'swam and explored rock pools' and, 'played tennis with other teenagers.'[2] Here they were joined by friends Gordon and Ida Biggs (neighbours, who lived at Upton Leigh, next door to Green Hedges) and their children, who persuaded Enid and Kenneth to travel with them on holiday to the USA; this they did later that year. Imogen now joined her sister Gillian at boarding school. Enid had published the first of her 'Noddy' books entitled *Little Noddy goes to Toyland* in 1949, which was the year that Gillian commenced at St Andrew's University, Fife, Scotland, where she read history.

In 1950, Enid's mother Theresa died. The two had not met in almost thirty years, and granddaughters Gillian and Imogen were not even aware of their grandmother's existence until after her death.[3]

A company was founded in March 1950 to manage Enid's business affairs. However, instead of bearing her name, as might have seemed appropriate, it bore the name of her husband, 'Darrell Waters Ltd'. In that year, Enid assigned the royalties earned from her book, *Before I go to Sleep*, to the Shaftesbury Society Babies' Home in Beaconsfield, which consequently benefited to the tune of several thousand pounds (and of which she later became chairman of the local board).[4] Imogen also mentions the Spastics Society and the Sunshine Home for Blind Babies as other organizations which Enid supported.

Twenty
FIVE FALL INTO ADVENTURE: KIMMERIDGE: THE CLAVELL TOWER

In *Five Fall into Adventure,* (published 1950), the children spend another holiday at 'Kirrin', home of George and her dog Timmy. They go down to swim at a place, 'where rocks jutted up from the beach, surrounded by limpet rock pools. Anne went to look for sea anemones in the [rock] pool. She liked the petal-like creatures that looked so like plants and weren't. She liked feeding them with bits of biscuit, seeing their "petals" close over the fragments and draw them quickly inside.' [P.29.] The children row around the coast, rounding a high cliff on top of which was a, 'dour, grey stone building… a little like a small castle. It brooded over the sea, with one square tower overlooking the waves.'[1]

In *Five Fall into Adventure,* the description of rock pools is evocative of Kimmeridge Bay (near the tiny hamlet of Kimmeridge, 7 miles to the west of Swanage); just as the stone building which 'brooded over the sea' is evocative (at any rate as far as location is concerned), of Kimmeridge's Clavell Tower. This is a folly, constructed in 1831 and situated above the bay on the cliff top, with fine views of the English Channel.

The Clavell Tower.

65

Twenty One

THE RUBADUB MYSTERY: LULWORTH COVE: PORTLAND HARBOUR

*T*he *Rubadub Mystery* (published 1951) concerns not 'The Famous Five', but four different children: Barney, Roger, Diane and Snubby, who find themselves on holiday at a, 'dear little old fashioned seaside village' with, 'a pier… and a promenade, and plenty of things going on.' The journey involves, 'many long stops at various [railway] stations…' until finally they arrive at 'Rubadub' and the 'Three Men in a Tub Inn' where they are to stay in a room that looked, 'down a steep cliff-side to the golden sands below. "This place has got a lovely old feel," said Diana, and Roger agreed. "You can feel that things have happened here for years – the walls still remember them!" "There used to be smugglers here in the old days," said Snubby. There is also mention of the, 'little private beach belonging to the hotel.'[1]

The children's peace is shattered when, as they are asleep at the inn, there is a terrific booming noise. 'The inn shook, Snubby sat up in bed, scared. Bombs! he thought,' (a clear allusion to the war.) However, Snubby decides that the booming noise has a different origin. 'It's an explosion in the submarine bay,' he says. Shortly afterwards he notices searchlights, 'playing here and there,' and, 'criss-crossing….'[2] (Another unmistakable image of wartime.)

They are taken by a boatman to see a blow-hole, and he proceeds to explain what it is:

> 'Haven't you ever seen one before? There's plenty round our coasts, some big, some little. There's a long passage through the rocks from the whirlpool to the blow-hole, and when it's high tide, as it is now, the whirlpool waters get sucked down, and some of them are forced by the tide and the suction through the passage and out of the blow-hole. Watch – there'll be another spout in a minute.'

The boatman also takes them to a rocky promontory, from which they can see over the 'submarine bay':

'You know what goes on there I don't doubt,' said the boatman. 'Secret submarine work. No one's allowed there, not even us fishermen, though as a boy, I knew every corner. A stone enclosure guarded the whole of the bay. No ships could get in or out without the secret openings being unlocked. Men kept guard in little stone shelters along the top.'[3]

Stair Hole, Lulworth.

From the description, it is tempting to think that the village of 'Rubadub' in *The Rubadub Mystery* is in fact Swanage (despite the fact that the inn was situated on a 'steep cliff side'). Also that the 'little private beach' [RD p.236] referred to was proba-bly either the one which belonged to the Hotel Grosvenor, or the small beach at nearby Buckshore (which is a favourite of local Swanage people, even to this day). As regards the blow-hole, a feature similar to the one in the story (and known in real life as Stair Hole) is to be found immediately to the west side of Lulworth Cove. Here, the sea has excavated a cavernous system behind the outer limestone barrier of rocks; as the waves come gushing in at several points, turbulence occurs and a geyser-like effect is created.

Most intriguing of all, however, is the 'submarine bay', which has its paral-lel in Portland Harbour, a place also associated with submarines, as will shortly be seen. Is it purely a coincidence that just as in the fictional *Rubadub Mystery*, the 'submarine bay' can be seen from the vicinity of the blow-hole, so in real life, Portland Harbour is visible (on a clear day) from the vicinity of Stair Hole?

Portland is a rocky peninsula, about 2 miles in width, which extends some 4½ miles into the English Channel. Construction of its harbour commenced in 1847, in order to provide a shelter for shipping and act as a defence against would-be French invaders. In fact, the breakwater was constructed by prisoners, who came to the island the following year and were accommodated at Portland Prison, newly built for the purpose. Portland Harbour, which is 2107 acres in size and took twenty-three years to construct, subsequently became the headquarters of the Royal Navy's Channel Fleet.

Portland Harbour   Photo: Tony Campbell.

The 'secret submarine work' which in *The Rubadub Mystery* was carried out in the 'submarine bay' brings to mind the fact that it was at Portland where torpedoes were developed and manufactured.

Twenty Two
QUAY, PIER AND PADDLE STEAMERS

From the terrace of the Hotel Grosvenor, Enid would have had an excellent view of both of Swanage's piers. Enid's daughter Gillian recalls taking a paddle steamer from Swanage pier to Bournemouth pier, 'for an autographing session [i.e. book signing], with her mother.'[1]

Before either of Swanage's two piers were built, goods and passengers were obliged to disembark at the stone sea wall. However, in 1823, a dedicated stone quay was built for the purpose. This was before the advent of the railway, when such items as coals, building materials, and foodstuffs had to be brought to Swanage by sea.

The Swanage Pier Act of 1859 authorized the construction of a wooden pier, 750 feet in length, and on 3 November of that year, the first vessel to dock, the *Purveyor* of Southampton, arrived to unload its cargo of 50 tonnes of rails and a quantity of timber with which to build the adjacent tramway.[2]

The paddle steamer Majestic.
Photo: David Haysom Collection.

By the autumn of the following year, the pier was fully open to traffic with its four landing stages.

Prior to 1880, what was described as a, 'fitful, sporadic, loss-making and generally uncomfortable steamer service, had operated between Bournemouth pier and Swanage.' In that year however, a new

69

promenade, steamer and pleasure pier was constructed. This provided not only three steamer berths, but also a raised promenade deck 50 feet wide, equipped with, 'handsome, sheltered seats', together with changing rooms and springboards, 'for those who would enjoy a morning header [i.e. a dive into the water].' As a result, the steamer service underwent a great revival, and by 1884, so many tourists were arriving in Swanage by sea (18,000 in that year) that it became necessary for the pier to be enlarged. Within a decade, this number had risen to an astonishing 100-110,000.[3]

Twenty Three
GOLF

In 1951, the Isle of Purbeck Golf Club at Dean Hill, Studland, was purchased by Enid's company, Darrell Waters Ltd, and here, over the next few years, Enid and Kenneth were to enjoy many games of golf together. The club came into existence in the following way:

Dean Cottage was a thatched property, situated on the lower slopes of Dean Hill on the south side of the Studland to Corfe Castle road, and described as 'picturesque... with surrounding garden.'[1] This was the home of Thomas Howe, an agricultural labourer, and his wife Mary Ann. It was their son Joseph, who having spent some years in the USA, returned to Studland and created, in the vicinity of the cottage, a nine-hole golf course, namely the Isle of Purbeck Golf Links, which opened for play in 1893. A corrugated iron club house was subsequently erected beside the cottage, which became known affectionately as 'the little tin hut.'[2]

Joseph, who was now married and living at Dean Cottage with his parents, was appointed the club's professional, his wife Ellen preparing and serving the teas.[3] Later, Joseph's son Edward, who lived in an adjacent cottage on the hill, became the assistant professional.

Dean Cottage, with 'Little Tin Hut' and (left) Edward Howes' Cottage.

Photo: Johnny James.

Permission was obtained in 1924 from the club's landlord, Henry John Ralph Bankes Esq. (known as Ralph, owner of the Kingston Lacy and Corfe Castle Estates), for the creation of further holes on Godlingston Heath (on the north side of the Studland to Corfe Castle road). Bankes duly became the club's first president. With the advent of war in 1939, some of the golf course's land was requisitioned by the military.

Enid and Kenneth at the Isle of Purbeck Golf Club.

Photo: Isle of Purbeck Golf Club Ltd.

The takeover of the club by Darrell Waters Ltd in 1951 solved the problem of the club's members being unable to afford to pay the costs required to restore those holes which had now been relinquished by the military. In Gillian's words, 'Kenneth and my mother were delighted to take the course over and turn it back into an 18-hole course again.'

Enid, with Kenneth's encouragement, had by now become a proficient golfer. She was duly elected ladies' captain, and she donated a prize for a golf competition, to be held the following spring. At this time, the club's professional was Harry Sales of Studland village, whose wife Freda was stewardess.

From the age of twelve, Gordon James of Swanage, known as Johnny, had spent his spare time working at the golf club, mowing the grass with a 'Pennsylvania mower' (in the days before petrol-driven mowers were available, and hand-mowers were used to cut the grass), for the sum of ninepence per hour. Soon, however, he discovered that he could earn more money as a caddy, for which he was paid two shillings and sixpence per hour, and this is how, in 1948 when he was aged eighteen, he came to meet Enid and her family. Kenneth now appointed Johnny to be permanent greenkeeper. Little did he suspect that soon, he would feature as a character in one of Enid's books!

When Johnny became Enid's caddy, he remarked that she was, 'very good on the tipping; she always used to give me five shillings a day, which in the 1950s was a lot of money.' Enid was in the habit of playing an astonishing three and a half rounds of golf per day (or 63 holes), a prodigious feat which would have taken approximately eight hours to perform, and involved climbing up many gradients on the undulating course. At other times, Enid would sit and write her letters, in the shade of the trees adjacent to what was then the 16th hole.

Johnny also caddied for Kenneth, a stickler for the etiquette of the game, who picked him up at his front door in the black Rolls Royce, and always provided a packed lunch. In Johnny's words, Kenneth was 'golf crazy!' and took a childlike delight in finding lost balls and collecting discarded tees;

so much so that Enid would contrive with Johnny surreptitiously, to scatter tees around the course for Kenneth to find!

In later years, Johnny would take Kenneth's place for the latter holes as Enid's playing partner, when Kenneth became tired. 'If you keep the ball straight,' he told Johnny, 'I shall give you five shillings.' For a two-handicap golfer, which Johnny was, this was not a problem. 'They were a lovely couple with two lovely children,' he said.

Enid would later immortalize Johnny in her book *Five have a Mystery to Solve*, as the character 'Lucas', who was described as, 'nut brown, bright-eyed, telling stories of the animals and birds he loved so much.' And how did Johnny react to this news? 'I'm only an ordinary working person,' he said, 'but I feel highly honoured to be called "Lucas" in Enid Blyton's books.'[4]

Enid took a keen interest in the wide variety of flora and fauna to be found in the vicinity of the golf course. For example, gentians, bee orchids, and also spotted orchids grew wild between the seventh and eighth tees. This love of nature, which Enid had shared with her father Thomas, stemmed from her childhood days, when she went with him for long walks in the woods and fields.[5] Also to be seen in the vicinity were various creatures, such as deer, foxes, rabbits, and reptiles: adders, sand lizards, and even smooth snakes, which were all native to the heathland on which the golf course was built.

This interest of Enid's was reflected by her writing a total of 31 nature books. Some, such as *The Zoo Book*, *The Children's Garden* (now called *Let's Garden*) and *Round the Year with Enid Blyton* were purely factual; others, such as *Hedgerow Tales*, *Rambles with Uncle Nat*, and the *Jinky Nature Books* were written in story format. It would surely have pleased her greatly to know that the land to the east of the Godlingston course is now a national nature reserve.

Twenty Four

'KIRRIN COTTAGE':
'HILL COTTAGE': REAL-LIFE COTTAGES

In 'The Famous Five' stories, George's home, 'Kirrin Cottage', is in the village of Kirrin. Julian, Dick and Anne have often stayed here during their holidays, and now their own family has moved to the same vicinity.

In *Five on a Treasure Island*, written in 1941 and published the following year, 'Kirrin Cottage' is described as being too small for, 'Mother and Daddy to stay the night' (i.e. in addition to the children), and as having windows which, 'looked over the moors at the back of the house, [with] one side-window [which] looked over the sea….' There is, 'a farm a little way off….'[1] Many such cottages fitting this description exist, not only in Purbeck but also elsewhere.

In *Five have a Mystery to Solve*, written in 1961 and published a year later, there is mention of another dwelling, 'Hill Cottage', which is situated near to 'Kirrin Cottage', and is the home of Mrs Layman (a friend of the mother of Julian, Dick and Anne). 'Hill Cottage' is described as, 'a dear little house upon the hills, overlooking the harbour… [with] funny little chimneys, rather crooked walls, a thatched roof, all uneven [and] tiny windows.' There is, 'no water laid on, only just a well to use – and no electricity or gas – just candles or an oil lamp.'[2]

In Chapter 3 of *Five have a Mystery to Solve*, the children's journey to Mrs Layman's 'Hill Cottage' is clearly described: 'They went along a road that ran on the top of a hill. They swung round a corner – and there, spread far below them, was a great sea vista that included a wonderful harbour, filled with big and little ships.' Those familiar with Purbeck will be instantly reminded, by this description, of the real-life view of Poole Harbour and Brownsea Island obtainable from the viewpoint on the Corfe to Studland Road. That this is no coincidence is confirmed by Enid, who in a 'Special Note' states that 'Whispering Island', mentioned in the story, which is 'set in the great blue harbour… is real'. Enid also confirms that: 'The little cottage on the hills is still there, with its magnificent view and its old well, and Lucas [based on her golfing caddy Johnny James] can be found on the golf course, nut-brown and bright-eyed, telling stories of the animals and birds he loves so much.' So where might this real-life cottage be situated?

Chapter 6 of *Five have a Mystery to Solve* includes a description of how the golf course (presumably the Isle of Purbeck) is reached from 'Hill Cottage':

> The [Famous] Five... went up the hill, crossed over the road that ran along the top, and climbed over a stile. They found themselves on one of the fairways of the golf course not far from the green, in which stood a pole with a bright red flag waving at the top.[3]

It so happens that there is a dwelling in the area which would fit this location, namely Agglestone Cottage. Built of Purbeck stone in about 1840, with a roof of slate (never thatch), it is situated in a copse adjacent to the east side of the eighth fairway of the main Godlingston course. Agglestone Cottage also has a well, as Enid described, but without the conventional bucket and chain mechanism. Instead, its water was conveyed to the kitchen by means of a pipe, through which it flowed under the force of gravity. In forty years the well was only known to run dry twice!

In Enid's time, Agglestone Cottage was occupied by Mrs Margaret Tubb, who worked as a cleaning lady at the golf club, and on one occasion was presented with the gift of a Poole Pottery vase by Enid herself (as was Freda, wife of Harry Sales, the club's professional). Margaret, born and bred in Corfe Castle, was married to George Tubb, and Agglestone Cottage was her home for forty years (up until 1987). The couple had three children, who were taken to school in Swanage by bus (where George worked for a builders' and plumbers' merchant.)

By a strange coincidence, there is a connection between the Tubb family, the local clay industry, and Enid's story, *Five go to Mystery Moor*, as will shortly be demonstrated.

Twenty Five
CHRIS RONE: 'MR [PC] PLOD'

Enid's time at the Isle of Purbeck Golf Club brought her into contact with a real-life character – a policeman – who inspired her to call one of the characters in her books, also an officer of the law, 'Mr Plod'.

PC Chris Rone in Weymouth.

Photo: Barbara Haines.

Christopher Raymond Rone (Chris) was born in Leigh, Worcestershire in 1915, the second year of the First World War. Before, and during the Second World War, he served for eight years in the Grenadier Guards, being billeted in Park Road, Swanage and elsewhere in the area before serving overseas. It was in Swanage that he met his wife-to-be, Barbara Joan Clark, who worked in a grocery store in the town and whom he married on 25 June 1942. Finally, having been demobilized at the end of the war, Chris rejoined his wife to make a new life in the Isle of Purbeck as a member of the Dorset Police Constabulary.

It was during his time spent on the beat at Studland – where he was stationed from 1952-56 – that Chris struck up an acquaintanceship with Enid Blyton whose company, Darrell Waters Ltd, had purchased the Isle of Purbeck Golf Club the previous year. Enid told Swanage reporter George Willey that PC Rone, who at that time lived in the police house at Studland, used to walk in a rather stately way around the village. 'As I watched him,' she said, 'the name came into my mind, and I decided to call my character PC Plod.'[1] As Chris himself recalled:

> She [Enid] once told me that she had based her character PC Plod on me. She used to see me a lot in the village [i.e. Studland] but it all began with me pushing my pedal cycle up that steep hill to the golf course where she often would be

playing. This gave her the idea of calling a policeman character in her ['Noddy'] children's books Mr Plod, though I
certainly didn't resemble the character in any other way. [This
was certainly true, Chris being tall, handsome, and sporting a
Hollywood-style moustache.]

Chris's former colleague Bert Beavis said, 'I'm not surprised Enid Blyton
used him as PC [Mr] Plod. He [Chris] was friendly, pleasant and liked by
everyone – the typical village "bobby" of his day.'

✧ ✧ ✧

Although a policeman appears in the very first 'Noddy' book in the series,
entitled (apart from the first imprint) *Noddy goes to Toyland* (published in

1949 by Sampson Low), it is not
until *Well Done, Noddy* appears in
1952 that this policeman assumes
the name 'Mr Plod'. (Toyland is
where Noddy lives, along with a
series of other characters who
include Big Ears, Mrs Tubby Bear,
Wobbly Man, Mickey Monkey
and of course, Mr [PC] Plod.
Noddy drives an open-top yellow
and red two-seater car.)

'Noddy' and 'Mr Plod'.

Photo: Linda Appleby.

✧ ✧ ✧

Did Chris object to being the inspiration for the name 'Mr Plod', who
featured in the vast majority of the 154 'Noddy' stories which subsequently
sold millions of copies throughout the world? The answer is quite the
opposite. 'I thought he [Chris] would be offended in some way,' said
reporter George Willey, 'but to my amazement he was delighted, and spent
the rest of his life boasting to people that he was the prototype of Mr Plod.'
This view is confirmed by Chris's daughter Barbara Haines:

Dad was very proud that he was in the 'Noddy stories', but far
too modest to make it public. The family knew [i.e. about the
relationship between Chris and Mr Plod] and we avidly read
all the 'Noddy' books, but he always said he would have been

embarrassed if his colleagues found out. (In fact, Enid agreed to keep the association between Chris and Mr Plod secret, for this very reason.)

PC Rone's service record presents a picture of a dedicated and courageous officer, who received the following commendations:

JANUARY 1947: Commended (with others) for work in connection with a case of cinema break in, [in] Swanage.
MAY 1954: Commended by letter from the Assistant Chief Constable for action taken in effecting a cliff rescue at Swanage.
SEPTEMBER 1956: Commended (with others) by letter from the Chief Constable for assistance rendered at a cliff rescue at Swanage.
JUNE 1965. Commended (with one other) for initiative and astute police duty leading to the arrest of Francis John Cook on 29 April 1965 for the larceny of a motor car.
MAY 1968. [Awarded] Police Long Service and Good Conduct Medal.[2]

In all, 154 'Noddy' books (illustrated by the Dutch artist Eelco Martinus ten Harmsen van der Beek) were published. With the growing demand for 'Noddy' memorabilia (which included a clockwork 'Noddy', a 'Mr Plod' egg cup, a 'Noddy' snakes and ladders game, a 'Noddy' jigsaw puzzle, and even 'Noddy' soap and toothpaste) Enid, 'carefully checked every design for 'Noddy' merchandise just as she had always checked every piece of art work for her books,' said Gillian.[2] Within little over a decade, sales of 'Noddy' books would reach in excess of 26 million copies. Meanwhile, in the real world, as it were, life went on.

Twenty Six
THE EARLY 1950s

Enid and Kenneth continued to spend three holidays a year at Swanage's Hotel Grosvenor; two of which were taken during school term-time (i.e. without the children). Each would last for a period of two weeks. For Gillian, now in her second year at university, 1951 would mark her final holiday at Swanage with the family. This would be taken, as usual, at the Hotel Grosvenor. From 1952, however, the family holidayed at Swanage's Grand Hotel.

'In the early 1950s,' said Imogen, 'my mother became much more involved in public appearances and duties.' This included story-telling and auto-graphing sessions. In response to demands from her child readers, Enid founded The Famous Five Club in September 1952, to be run by her publisher, Hodder & Stoughton. Her agreement for this, however, was conditional on the subscribers participating in fundraising activities, in support of the Shaftesbury Society's Children's Home in Beaconsfield (of which Enid became chairman of the local board). From 1953, news of the club's members, and of the children's home, was published in the newly created *Enid Blyton Magazine*. In its heyday, the club boasted over a million members, and raised sufficient money to fund a cot in the Great Ormond Street Hospital for Sick Children, and a minibus for the Stoke Mandeville Hospital for Spinal Injuries.

In 1953 (the year of the coronation of Queen Elizabeth II), at Enid's sugges-tion, the Sunbeam Society was formed, in aid of the Sunshine Homes for Blind Babies, and within six years the yellow badge of the society was worn by, 'over 22,000 of my warmest-hearted and generous readers.'[1]

In Swanage, Enid was elected President (Honorary) of the Regatta and Carnival Committee, a promoter of good causes, a post that she held for the following three years.

✧ ✧ ✧

Kenneth suffered increasingly from arthritis of the joints, so much so that in his latter years at the Isle of Purbeck Golf Club, he was obliged to use a golf buggy – red in colour, and referred to by Johnny James as a 'Noddy car' – to negotiate the course. He would drive up to the tee, which he would then approach on crutches before playing his shot.[2] Meanwhile, the Godlingston Heath course was extended to a full 18 holes, with the original Dean Hill course being reduced to nine holes.

In 1954, *Noddy in Toyland* was produced as a pantomime. In December that year, Enid resigned from her directorship of the company Darrell Waters Limited (which had been created in 1950 to manage her financial affairs). Imogen believed that the reason for this could have been,

> …the attitude of the other directors towards my mother's charitable interests. They were quite happy for her to raise money from children and adults for charity, as she had been doing with quite unprecedented success since the 1930s, but it was quite a different matter for her to give large sums of her own money, for example the royalties from a book, which deprived the company of valuable income. My mother had dug deep into her own pocket in the 1940s for charities concerned with children in need. My mother was a natural giver, and children with disability aroused in her a deep compassion.[3]

In the same year, Enid became chairman of The Famous Five Club's committee. By now, her books had been translated into many European languages.

Twenty Seven
FIVE GO TO MYSTERY MOOR

In *Five go to Mystery Moor* (published 1954) there are descriptions of mists rolling in from the sea, and of, 'great stretches of wiry grass, masses of heather springing up afresh, and blazing its gold everywhere on this lovely April day, was the gorse.'

As 'The Famous Five' ride out on 'Mystery Moor', in company with an accomplished rider called 'Henry' (Henrietta), Anne makes a discovery as she scrapes away at some heather. 'It seems like rails or something,' said Henry. 'Very old and rusty.' Julian confirms that this is the case, but asks, 'But what in the world were rails laid down here for?' A blacksmith called 'Old Ben' tells the children that a family called 'Bartle', having discovered plentiful supplies of 'good sharp sand' in the vicinity, 'set to work and built a little railway and trucks to the (sand) quarry and back.' The Bartles, however, quarrelled with some travellers (formerly called gypsies) who lived on the moor, and the latter, 'pulled up bits of the line, here and there, and the little engine toppled over and pulled the trucks with it.' Finally, 'The Five' return in search of the engine (locomotive) and duly find it.

Given the fact that so many of 'The Famous Five' books appear to be founded, as far as location is concerned, to a greater or lesser extent in reality, it is reasonable to enquire, is there a 'moor' in Purbeck, and if so did it feature a disused railway line? (As Gillian remarked, 'That countryside was part of my mother and her imagination.'[1]) In fact the answer, which does not come as a complete surprise, is yes, on both counts.

When Enid played her rounds of golf at the Isle of Purbeck Golf Club, or sat in the clubhouse, or on the downs there writing her books, her view from this lofty position would have been of open moorland – stretching all the way to Poole Harbour. Across the moorland once ran a railway, or to be more accurate, a tramway, which was used not for transportation of passengers, but by the mining industry. The commodity which was mined here, however, and which led to the laying down of the (narrow gauge) railway, was not sand, as in the story, but clay, highly desirable not only in its own right, but also on account of the strength and plasticity which it imparts to other clays when mixed with them.

In 1760, William Pike, then aged thirty-one, from a Devon clay-mining and shipping family, took up residence in Market Place, Corfe Castle, together with, 'a writing clerk… to whom he paid 12s a week,' three clay-cutters and a woman servant.[2] He and his brother Joseph founded a company, W.J. and J.W. Pike (or Pike Brothers) and mining activities expanded rapidly.

Open-cast clay mines at Norden.
Photo: William Stockley.

A rival of Pike Brothers was London merchant Benjamin Fayle, who owned clay pits at Norden, near Corfe Castle. It was Fayle who, in 1806, built Purbeck's first narrow gauge railway (tramway), which initially used horse-drawn waggons, and later steam loco-motives to transport the clay across Middlebere Heath (of which Hartland Moor is part) to Middlebere in the Wareham Channel. (Prior to this, clay had been transported by pack horse.)

In 1830 Pike Brothers, not to be outdone, built their first railway, which ran from Furzebrook, two miles to the west of Corfe Castle) to Ridge Wharf, on the Wareham Channel. Soon a network of railways served Purbeck's dozens of open-cast clay mines.

In Enid's time, the route of disused Fayle's Tramway, 2 miles to the north, would have been clearly visible as it ran across Rempstone and Newton Heaths (For the great treee plantations were not created until the late 1950s.) Not only that, but at least one of the old steam, narrow gauge loco-motives was also still to be seen in the vicinity. This was 'Tiny', whose

The Blue Pool.
Photo: Joan Barnard.

chimney Enid may well have seen sticking out of the scrubland at Norden, where she lay for many years before being disman-tled for scrap.[3]

In *Five go off in a Caravan* (published in 1946) there is mention of, 'an enormous, blue lake that lay glittering in the August sunshine;' and in *Five on a Hike Together* (published in 1951), of another lake that is, 'a wonderful dark blue'. Could Enid, when describing these lakes, have had in her mind's eye the Blue Pool at Furzebrook (2 miles west of Corfe Castle), formerly one of Pike Brothers' open-cast clay mines, which in her time had become (and still remains) a tourist attraction? (Historically, when a mine was exhausted, it naturally filled with water to form a lake.)

The popularity of the Blue Pool resides in the spectacular colour changes to be observed in its waters, from a deep blue, to turquoise or emerald green. This is the consequence of light of varying intensity diffracting from the minuscule particles of clay suspended in its still depths.

Finally, were there travellers on (or in the vicinity of) Hartland Moor, just as there were on 'Mystery Moor'? According to Miss Jennifer Barnard, proprietor of the Blue Pool, yes, most certainly, in the shape of the Hughes family, who with their horses and caravans were encamped for many years, near to the exit road.

Mention has been made of a link between Agglestone Cottage, the clay industry and the narrow gauge railway. This is that the ancestors of George Tubb, who lived at the cottage with his wife Margaret, during the time of Enid's ownership of the Isle of Purbeck Golf Club, were employed as engine drivers on Benjamin Fayle's Norden to Goathorn railway.

By the mid-1950s, the tramways were largely abandoned in favour of road transportation. However, for at least another two decades, remnants of the industry, such as disused locomotives, wagons, engine sheds, and track were still to be seen.

Bill Tubb and his Fayle Company locomotive.
Photo: Margaret Tubb.

Twenty Eight
FIVE ON A SECRET TRAIL

In *Five on a Secret Trail* (published 1956), mention is made of a common, with heather, pine trees, adders and streams, which is within walking distance of the village of 'Kirrin', where there was once, 'an old Roman camp.' (This common is in some ways reminiscent of the one at Corfe Castle.) Here the children befriend Guy Lawdler, whose father is a famous explorer and archaeologist. Guy tells them that he has discovered pottery, weapons, and several old coins on the site of the camp; also, 'an old brooch, a long pin-like thing, and part of a stone head [i.e. bust].'[1] What gave Enid the idea of writing a story involving archaeology and the Romans?

Maiden Castle.   Photo: Tony Campbell.

The most famous archaeologist of the time, and arguably of all time, was Sir Mortimer Wheeler, about whose exploits Enid would most certainly have been aware from the newspapers. In fact, between 1934 and 1938, Sir Mortimer had come to Dorset to excavate the great and ancient hillfort of Maiden Castle, two miles south-west of Dorchester.

In the course of his excavations, Sir Mortimer discovered evidence of a brutal battle that had taken place in about AD44 between the Roman invaders and the indigenous British defenders. A cache of some 25,000 pebbles was unearthed, originating from the Chesil Beach and used by the defenders as sling shot; also numerous iron arrowheads, scattered over the ground having been fired by the attackers. In what was evidently

Sir Mortimer Wheeler.

Photo: Crown Copyright.

a war cemetery, were 38 skeletons of men and women; in one, a ballista arrowhead (i.e one which had been fired mechanically, by a crossbow) was found embedded in his spinal vertebrae, and the skulls of others bore the marks of extensive sword lacerations.[2]

Sir Mortimer was a frequent visitor to Enid's home town of Beaconsfield, which was also the home of his sister Betty. Furthermore, there was an even closer connection between Enid's family and that of the Wheelers', in that Betty's son Peter, when he was an undergraduate at Cambridge University in the mid-1950s, had been the boyfriend of Enid's daughter Imogen, and they had attended a May Ball together.

Enid's pleasure at the prospect of a visit to Swanage never palled, and is evident in the *Adventure of the Strange Ruby* (published 1960), where she for once chooses to identify both Swanage and Corfe Castle by their real names. 'We're going somewhere for the hols,' says Faith. 'If only it was Swanage again!'[3] Swanage is described in the story as, 'just the same as ever – a great wide bay of forget-me-not blue, with hardly a ripple or a wave, except just at the edge. Behind rose the glorious hills.'[4] As for Corfe Castle, 'The two [Pat and Tessa] cycled off. They took the Corfe Castle direction and marvelled, as always, when they came to the ancient little village, dominated by the centuries-old ruined castle, dreaming by itself high up on the hill.'[5]

As to the fortunes of Enid and her family, the Enid Blyton Magazine Club was created in 1956 with the aim of helping young children with muscular spasticity caused by cerebral palsy. It was soon to have over 150,000 subscribers.

In August 1957, Gillian married Donald Baverstock (a producer for the BBC) at St James' Church, Picadilly. In the same year, Kenneth retired as senior surgeon at St Stephen's Hospital, Fulham. Meanwhile, Imogen at St Andrew's University, switched from classics, to read philosophy and economics instead.[6]

Twenty Nine

FIVE ON FINNISTON FARM

First published in 1960, this story is set not on the coast but inland. It begins with Julian and Dick cycling to the top of a hill while, 'below them [is] spread the Dorset countryside, shimmering in the heat of the day...'[1] Their objective is to meet the bus bringing Anne, George, and Timmy the dog to Finniston Church, before going on to Finniston Farm, which is owned by a Mr Trevor Philpot and his wife; the latter being an old school friend of George's mother, who takes in paying guests. The Philpots have two children, Harry and Harriet, who are twins.

They arrive to find that the farmhouse is very old, with, 'beams running across the walls and into the roof.' Lodging with Mrs Philpot is an American boy Junior, and his father Mr Henning, to whom Mrs Philpot has sold, 'some of her own things' because, 'she just had to have some money....'[2] It is decided that the girls should sleep in the farmhouse, and Julian and Dick in the great barn at the rear.

In the village's ice cream shop/baker's/dairy, they meet Janie, whose Uncle Bill works on the farm. In the antique shop they meet an old man called Mr Finniston, who tells them that he is a descendant of the owners of the local castle – which was burnt down – and to which Finniston Farm belonged. The story is that when the castle was attacked, traitors within its gates set fire to it, and while the castle folk were fighting the fire, the enemy walked in and slew nearly all of them. The old chapel, however, escaped the fire and was now used as a storehouse for grain. 'Sad, sad,' said Mr Finniston but, 'mind you – it's still full of prayer'.[3] (i.e. the chapel still has an atmosphere of prayer.)

The children are intrigued when Mr Finniston alludes to the fact that within the castle's cellars and dungeons, there may be, 'the bones of prisoners... chests of money,' or, 'things stored away by the lady of the castle.' The American gentleman, Mr Henning, brings a Mr Richard Durleston to look around the farm and the old chapel, because the latter, 'knows more about houses in England than anyone else in the country.'[4]

Hoping to find the site of the castle, the children are fortunate when Snippit, the twin's black poodle, disappears down a rabbit hole, and comes up with an oyster shell. He is then joined by Timmy, who brings up more shells and a collection of small and large bones. They then realize that they have discovered the site of the castle's kitchen midden (rubbish dump). Their conversation is overheard by the American boy Junior, who rushes back to tell his father the news. Mr Herring then offers Mr and Mrs Philpot a cheque for £5000 for the rights to begin excavating the site, and they begin work on a, 'shallow basin… [a] light depression near the summit of the hill.'[5]

Working on the assumption that the lady of the castle must somehow have escaped from its cellars to the chapel, the children go in search of the underground tunnel that she would have used. They have another piece of good fortune when Snippit chases a friendly jackdaw – known to the twins as Nosey – down a rabbit hole. This time he comes up with an ancient carved dagger. The children now realize that they have found the tunnel which they are looking for. Further exploration reveals a large, under-ground storeroom containing suits of armour and two chests; one of which is full of gold pieces, and the other of jewellery.

On their return journey they are trapped by a landslip, and so choose to return via the main tunnel which leads them to the chapel. Here, Bill releases them by lifting the trap door. Finally, the American Mr Henning is sent packing, and the Philpots now have enough money from what they will receive from the Crown (for their 'treasure trove') to purchase two new tractors and a new Land Rover.

Enid made no secret of the fact that she based Finniston Farm on Manor Farm at Stourton Caundle in North Dorset, which she purchased in 1956 as a going concern, even though she did not choose to live there. According to Gillian, her parents were advised to buy the farm by a Mr Flower, owner of a large sheep farm near Salisbury.[6]

Although Manor Farm was built early in the eighteenth century, the nearby chapel dates from the thirteenth century, and was described in 1970 by the

Royal Commission on Historical Monuments as: '...comprising a chancel and a nave, the chancel having lancet windows on each side and a wagon roof. At the time of writing however, "only the thirteenth century nave survives: it is used as a barn".'[7] This corresponds to 'the old chapel' as described in *Five on Finniston Farm*, and correlates with Enid's statement to Gillian that when she first saw the chapel, 'it was full of grain sacks with the cat and some kittens [sitting] on them.'

Manor Farm.   Photo: Oliver S.L. Simon.

Of particular interest is the question of whether or not there was ever a castle attached to the manor. About this there is some controversy. Historian, the Reverend John Hutchins, in his *History and Antiquities of the County of Dorset* (published 1774), quotes a Mr Coker as saying, 'John de Haddon had a little castle here,' and that, 'Sir William Stourton maintained the old castle for a removing house.' (Possibly a summer retreat.)[8] However, the Royal Commission on Historical Monuments presents a different view, stating that, 'There is no evidence of a mediaeval castle...' and that, 'the remains, which are situated 300 yards south-west of the church...' are probably those of 'a former manor house, perhaps with turrets...'.[9]

From 1960, Enid and Kenneth broke with tradition by transferring from Swanage's Grand Hotel to the Knoll House Hotel in Studland (owned by Colonel Kenneth Ferguson since the previous year) for their holidays.

Thirty
FIVE GO TO DEMON'S ROCKS: LIGHTHOUSES

The story (published in 1961) features a lighthouse which is owned by Tinker, the son of Professor Hayling, a friend of Quentin (the children's uncle and father of George – Georgina). The lighthouse, where 'The Famous Five' are to spend a holiday, is described as, 'wave-swept' and, 'a good way out from the shore.' An elderly gentleman named Jeremiah Boogle tells them that any ship that hugs the coast beyond a certain point would be, 'forced inland by the current, and thrown on those rocks down there – Demon's Rocks. And that's the end of them. No ship has ever been able to escape the sharp teeth of those wicked rocks, once she's caught in that current.'[1]

Lighthouses were probably something of a novelty for Enid Blyton, living as she did far from the sea. However, at Swanage (as previously mentioned) she found herself within a mile of the lighthouse at Anvil Point. Approval for the creation of this particular lighthouse was given a result of the shipwrecking of the vessel *Wild Wave* in 1875 (as also previously mentioned). It became operational on 28 September 1881, the ceremonial lighting of its oil lamp being performed by the then President of the Board of Trade.[2]

A lighthouse more similar to the one described in *Five go to Demon's Rocks* is that of The Needles, situated at the westernmost point of the Isle of Wight, where over a period of seven years, Enid, her first husband Hugh, and the children spent their holidays.

Thirty One

FIVE HAVE A MYSTERY TO SOLVE

In *Five have a Mystery to Solve* (published 1962), Julian, Dick and Anne (who now live with their parents near the village of 'Kirrin') are invited to spend another holiday at 'Hill Cottage', the home of an acquaintance Mrs Layman (as previously mentioned); this is so that Mrs Layman's grandson, Wilfred, will have some company while she herself goes away to visit a sick cousin.

It transpires that Wilfred is extremely fond of animals, as evidenced by the grass snake which he produces from his pocket. Wilfred also possesses pet beetles, a toad and a spider. Also, with a 'curious little pipe', he is able to summon hares, rabbits and even a magpie.[1] Wilfred is angry when George's dog Timmy frightens these creatures away, but soon warms to him when the latter puts his head on Wilfred's knee and looks up at him lovingly.

The story features an island, which Wilfred tells them once, 'belonged to a lonely old man [who] lived in a big house in the very middle of the wood…. People kept wanting to buy his island, and he had some kind of watchmen to keep people from landing on it. These watchmen were pretty fierce – they had guns.'[2] One of these watchmen was a man called 'Lucas', who now worked as groundsman at the golf club.

They meet Lucas, who tells them that the island is known as 'Wailing Island' because of the sound which the wind makes when it meets the high cliffs. Others call it 'Whispering Island' because of the sound of the wind in the trees:

> But most of us call it 'Keep-Away Island' – and that's the best name of all, for there's never been any welcome there, what with the dark cliffs, the cool rocks, and the dense wood.[3]

Lucas says that the man who owns the island is wealthy, and that he bought it for security reasons because he was afraid of being robbed. The house in which he lives is actually, 'a great castle, [set] right in the middle of the thick woods.' The stone used to build the castle was taken from an old quarry which is now part of the golf course. On the island there were said to be many beautiful treasures, including statues, 'some of gold', belonging to the old man. When the old man fell into disfavour with the king, the island was stormed, and he and his servants were killed, but the treasures were never found. An, 'old fellow and his wife' subsequently went to live there. 'They wouldn't allow anybody there, and it was they who kept the gamekeepers with guns to frighten away sightseers. They wanted peace and quiet for themselves and for all the wild life on the island...,' said Lucas. Since they died, and the island passed to their great nephew, it has been uninhabited, apart from two men who are there to, 'frighten off visitors'. [4]

The children decide to hire a boat, but on their first excursion they are swept up onto the shore of the island by the powerful tides. They catch sight of the two men, but manage to remain unseen themselves. However, when they return to the cove they find that their boat is missing.

In a shed in the wood the children find boxes containing beautifully carved statues. Behind the shed they discover an old well, and anxious to obtain water for themselves and for Timmy, they turn the handle to lower the bucket, which unfortunately becomes disengaged. There is no option now but for Dick to shin down the rope and retrieve it, which he does. However, in the depths of the well he discovers an iron door which he manages to force open. Inadvertently he has discovered the hiding place of the statues. Now they are joined by Wilfred, who has rowed over in another boat.

When Wilfred goes off on his own and is apprehended by the men, the children resolve to hide up in the trees. However, when Wilfred explains that he is visiting the island because he is an animal lover, and produces a hedgehog from his pocket to prove it, the men decide to release him.

Wilfred looks over the cliff and notices four men, who have evidently emerged from nearby caves. He tells 'The Five', who decide to explore, and find themselves walking along a secret passage which leads into the dungeons of the old castle. 'I wonder how many poor, miserable prisoners have been kept down here in the cold?' said Julian. It is here that they discover more statues, this time made of gold, whose faces have, 'slanting eyes' which gleam when they shine their torches on them. [5] There is also a golden bed with a carved gold headpiece and gold legs, and a set of precious animals carved out of green jade. Suddenly, they are discovered and incarcerated in the dungeon by the men, but they manage to escape through the old well. The story has a happy ending; Timmy the dog being instrumental in knocking one of the men out by leaping up at him.

As previously mentioned, Enid, in the Preface to the book, declares of 'Whispering Island' that, 'Yes, the island is real, and lies in the great harbour, still full of whispering trees.' And of course Lucas who, 'can be found on the golf course,' was based on Enid's caddy Mr Gordon 'Johnny' James. The inescapable conclusion, therefore, which is reinforced by Mrs Layman who tells the children that the harbour as seen from her cottage, 'is the second biggest stretch of water in the whole world,' is that 'Whispering Island' is based in Enid's imagination on Brownsea Island; and that her 'great harbour' is in fact Poole Harbour.

Thirty Two

BROWNSEA ISLAND

W hen striding out over the golf course, where she and Kenneth spent so much of their time, Enid's eyes would have been drawn downwards, across the great heathlands and forests, towards Poole Harbour and Brownsea Island.

Brownsea Island.

Photo: *Daily Echo*, Bournemouth.

Three-quarters of a square mile in area, Brownsea, situated near to the entrance of Poole Harbour, is the largest of its five principal islands. Yes, the island does have a castle, albeit not a ruined one such as is described in the books.

Brownsea (or Branksea) Castle, which overlooks Poole Harbour, was built during the reign of Henry VIII (1509-47) as part of a chain of coastal defences. During the Civil War (1642-51), the parliamentary forces strengthened the garrison and brought in extra ordnance. Since the time of the restoration of King Charles II (1660) the castle has been owned by a succession of private individuals.

Perhaps the most interesting of these was Charles van Raalte (of Dutch origin) who, in the spring of 1901, took up residence at the castle, together with his wife Florence. Charles, the beneficiary of the fortune which his father Marcus had made on the Stock Exchange, was the proud owner of the steam yacht *Maruja*, and of a superb collection of musical instruments.[1] He also created a nine-hole golf course on the island (of which Enid would undoubtedly have approved!) One of Charles' friends was the Italian inventor Guglielmo Marconi, who, from 1898-1926, conducted experiments in radio communication from The Haven Hotel on the mainland opposite.

As a keen naturalist herself, Enid would have been intrigued to read

Charles's book (published 1906, with illustrations by his wife Florence), entitled *Brownsea Island*. In it, he lists 81 varieties of fish known to have been caught off Brownsea Island including: blue shark; sea snake or pipe fish; flying fish (1893 and 1896); crayfish; porpoise, and a whale (washed up on the Hook Sands in 1894 – stranded afterwards on Boscombe beach.)[2] Also included is a list of 109 varieties of 'sea birds, water fowl and shore birds seen near Brownsea Island' including: kildeer plover; purple heron (seen near windmills in 1890 – indicating the presence of windmills on the island at this time); suacco heron; night heron; bittern; little bittern; purple sandpiper; king duck; Ross's gull. (All the aforementioned are described as 'very rare'.) As for 'land birds', 81 species are recorded: eagle (1892); merlin; hoopoe; Montagu's harrier; snow bunting; marsh harrier (1895) and hen harrier. However, it would have been a mistake to think of Charles as a conservationist, because following the appellation 'rare' or 'very rare' beside many of the entries, there appears the ominous word – 'shot'!

Brownsea Island is forever associated with Major General (later Lord) Robert Baden-Powell, who became a national hero following the defence of Mafeking by the British in the Second Boer War. In 1899 he wrote a military textbook, *Aids to Scouting* and, having discussed the idea with Charles and Florence van Raalte, it was here on the island that he held, between 25 July and 9 August 1907, his first ever scout camp. On that occasion 21 boys attended; some from public schools, and others from working-class families in Poole.[3]

The notion of 'Whispering Island' being a hostile and forbidding place in *Five have a Mystery to Solve* applies equally to Brownsea Island, which in 1927 was acquired by Mrs Mary Florence Bonham Christie, daughter of a banker and widow of an explorer and big game hunter. Having evicted the great majority of the islanders from their homes, from whence they returned to the mainland, this lady proceeded to set the island aside as a wild life sanctuary. Notices were put up forbidding any member of the public to set foot on the island, whose shoreline was now patrolled by guards.

Following the outbreak of war in September 1939, Brownsea Island (and all the other islands in Poole Harbour) was garrisoned by the military. Mrs Bonham Christie, however, continued to live there for the duration. (She died on 28 April 1961 aged ninety-six, having left Brownsea Island to her grandson John. The following year it was acquired by the National Trust.)

It is unlikely that Enid ever set foot on Brownsea Island, for the reasons stated above. Had she done so, she would have encountered a naturalist's paradise with rare red squirrels, hundreds of acres of purple flowering rhododendrons, a profusion of daffodils (the remnants of a former industry created in the days of the van Raaltes, with the object of supplying London's Covent Garden market) and the delightful church. There was also a large lagoon (formerly water meadows) created in 1853.

Thirty Three
BELIEFS

Enid's poem *April Day*, in a reference to Purbeck, describes how, 'So lavishly is beauty spread…,' that 'I must choose, to put away my shoes and kneel [i.e. pray] instead.'

Enid was baptized, brought up in the Christian faith (as a Baptist) and became a Sunday school teacher, with a great talent for relating the stories of the Bible to her young charges.

In her early years, there was so much that puzzled Enid about Christianity, that she decided she must write religious books in order, 'to tell the story of Christ so simply and clearly that even the youngest child would understand every word, and would see Jesus as a real, living person – someone who loved children, and who could tell the most wonderful stories in the world.' Also, 'I wanted to teach children how to pray, and I have written a book about that too. Prayer is a most important thing, and alas, thousands of parents nowadays don't teach their children this, and don't even know how to.'[1]

Some of the books published by Enid on the subject of Christianity include: *The Land of Far-Beyond* (1942 – a children's version of John Bunyan's *The Pilgrim's Progress*), *The Children's Life of Christ* (1943), *Tales from the Bible* (1944), *The Boy with the Loaves and Fishes* (1948), *The Children's Book of Prayers* (1953), *The Greatest Book in the World* (1954 – about the Bible), and the *Enid Blyton Bible Stories* (1949 and 1953 – for kindergarten children, comprising a total of 28 volumes!).

However, as the years passed, Enid came to view Christianity in a different light; telling Imogen that, 'she had learnt to see God as a threatening and angry masculine figure and clearly she in turn had been made angry by this projection.' As for the children, 'My mother taught me to say my prayers each night,' said Gillian. 'I went to church occasionally with my father [Hugh] when I was aged six. When I was seven, I continued to attend the church, which was Anglo-Catholic. I also sang in the choir.'

When Enid remarried, 'My stepfather [Kenneth] accompanied me to church at Christmas and Easter,'[2] said Imogen, 'My mother had left the Baptist faith of her childhood, and even though my sister and I were taken to church on some Sundays by a nanny, Christmas was a purely secular feast.'[3] Nevertheless, Gillian said, that Enid always knelt down beside her bed at night to say her prayers.

'I do believe in God, though perhaps not [in] your idea of God,' Enid told Dorothy Richards in 1935. 'I do trust Him in that I believe that there is a real purpose and love behind everything, and I do want to serve and love the Highest – whatever and whoever that may be. I would like a personal God like yours, but I find it difficult to believe in one that you can talk to as you do.'[4] Despite this, she insisted that her daughters were baptized into the Anglican faith, and also that they attended Sunday school.

'Then', said Imogen, 'my mother began rather hesitantly, to look at Roman Catholicism as a faith she might adopt,' but added:

> I suspect that she was envious of the comfort it brought to Dorothy, rather than interested in the faith itself. However, in spite of her separation from any religious observance in her adult life, the child within her very clearly had a strong faith.

This is evident in Enid's writing when, for example, in *The House at the Corner,* Pam declares that, 'she [i.e. Pam] had forgotten that prayers could bring comfort and peace,' and that, 'it was strange that how near God always seemed to be in a church….'[5]

Perhaps from this, one may conclude that Enid felt spiritually closer to God in the beautiful surroundings of such places as Dorset's Isle of Purbeck, rather than in the formal surroundings of a church.

Thirty Four

DECLINE

'For my mother,' said Imogen, 'a suspected heart attack at the time of my stepfather's retirement [1956] was followed by a series of deepening depressions and confusion that marks pre-senile dementia [Alzheimer's Disease – which adversely affects people's memory]. No one was able to help her face the gradual deterioration of her mind, which lasted for ten years.'[1] (Enid's mother Theresa had in her time also suffered from pre-senile dementia.)

In 1963, Enid and Kenneth sold Manor Farm, Stourton Caundle, to Oliver and Sue Simon. Sadly, the great tithe barn belonging to the farm was burnt down shortly afterwards, by children playing with matches (an episode of vandalism that would have horrified 'The Famous Five'). In that year, Enid wrote the last of 'The Famous Five' stories (namely *Five are Together Again*) by which time some six million copies of the series had been sold.

'She [Enid] was unable to write anything after 1963,' said Gillian, 'and her last three books were published the following year. I remember her saying to me at that time: "I'm finding it so difficult to read now, because I can't remember what I've just read".'[2]

In April 1965, the company, Darrell Waters Ltd, sold the Isle of Purbeck Golf Club to Mr Harry Beckham Randolph, former Chairman and Managing Director of the Wilkinson Sword Company. 'Gradually it became clear,' said Imogen, 'that the health of neither of them [i.e. Enid and Kenneth] was good enough to manage holidays, and [in 1966] the year before my stepfather died they stopped going [i.e. to the Knoll House Hotel, Studland].'[3]

Early in 1967, Enid telephoned her brother Hanly, with whom she had had no contact for almost seventeen years, to tell him she was 'desperately lonely', husband Kenneth having been admitted for a short stay in hospital. Kenneth died on 15 September 1967, aged seventy-five; after which time Enid was looked after by her housekeeper Doris Cox. Of Enid's love for Kenneth there was no doubt, for she afterwards wrote, 'I loved him so much. I feel lost and unhappy.'[4] Meanwhile, in the autumn of 1967, Imogen married bookseller Duncan Smallwood, and that December, Gillian and husband Donald, together with their four young children, moved to Yorkshire.

Finally, Enid was admitted to a nursing home in Hampstead at a time, said Gillian, 'when she could still recognize people close to her and remember something of her past.' She died peacefully in her sleep on 28 November 1968,[5] and was cremated at Golders Green in North London, in the presence of her family and close friends.

Thirty Five
CONCLUSION

In correspondence with Professor Peter McKellar during the 1950s, Enid tried to explain how she wrote her stories.

> When I begin a completely new book with new characters, I have no idea at all what the characters will be, where the story will happen, or what adventures or events will occur.
>
> I shut my eyes for a few minutes... I make my mind a blank and wait – and then, as clearly as I would see real children, my characters stand before me in my mind's eye. I see them in detail – hair, eyes, feet, clothes, expression – and I always know their Christian names but never their surname. More than that, I know their characters – good, bad, mean, gener-ous, brave, loyal, hot-tempered and so on.
>
> As I look at them, the characters take on movement and life.... Then behind the characters appears the setting, in colour, of course, of an old house – a ruined castle – an island – a row of houses. The story is enacted in my mind's eye almost as if I had a private cinema screen there. The characters come on and off, talk, laugh, sing – have their adventures – quarrel – and so on. I watch and hear everything, writing it down with my typewriter – reporting the dialogue... the expressions on the faces, the feelings of delight, fear, and so on.[1]

In his correspondence with Enid, McKellar uses the term 'Eidetic Imagery'; eidetic means having unusual vividness and detail, as if actually visible, and imagery refers to mental images which are the work of the imagina-tion.

For Enid, 'the imagery began as a young child' when, 'in bed, I used to shut my eyes and "let my mind go free".' And then, 'into it would come what I used to call my "night stories" – which were, in effect, all kinds of imaginings in story form....'[2] Such images are described as 'hypnogogic,' pertaining to a state of drowsiness preceding sleep.

> My imagination contains all the things I have ever seen or heard, things my conscious mind has long forgotten.... I don't think that I use anything I have not seen or experienced – I don't think I could. I don't think one can take out of one's mind more than one puts in.[3]

Enid referred to her sub-conscious as her 'under mind'. 'I knew how to get in touch with it. I knew how to be at one with it. I knew how to pull out the imaginings or put them into words.'[4] Gillian, in reference to *Five on a Treasure Island*, declared, 'I think that the things that we had seen down here [i.e. in Dorset] somehow percolated into that book,' and this is true of other 'Famous Five' books, as has been demonstrated.

For Enid, Dorset was a place she loved and enjoyed for holidays over many years; sharing this enjoyment with her two daughters and with her second husband Kenneth, and when in *Five have a Mystery to Solve*, Julian says, 'I somehow feel more English for having seen those Dorset fields, surrounded by hedges, basking in the sun,' this is surely a reflection of how Enid herself must have felt when she first saw them.[5]

However, while she was there, her conscious mind was committing images of the Dorset countryside and its people into her sub-conscious, exactly as she describes, to be 'got in touch with' later when they would reappear in her books, albeit 'transmuted, or formed into something that takes a natural and rightful place in the story,' where, 'I may recognise it, or I may not.'[6]

Enid's immense success as a writer may be measured by her output and sales: in excess of 700 books published during her lifetime, with approximately 400 million books sold worldwide and translated into more than 50 languages. In addition, Enid from the 1930s onwards, wrote approximately 5000 short stories;[7] also annuals, poetry books, song books, books of plays, the pantomime *Noddy in Toyland*, and the play *The Famous Five*.

However, just as her story and adventure books encouraged children to read, Enid also made a significant contribution to the field of children's education:

> 1926 – she wrote a substantial portion of and edited the 3-volume *Teachers' Treasury*.
> 1928 – she edited the 6-volume *Modern Teaching Practice for Juniors and Seniors*.
> 1930 – she was assistant editor for the 10-volume *Pictorial Knowledge*, of which she wrote the verse section.
> 1932 – she wrote part of and edited the 6-volume *Modern Teaching in the Infant School*.

Another facet of Enid's character was her immense generosity of spirit, which manifested itself when she became wealthy, and dedicated much of her fortune and time to charities working for the welfare of sick and disabled children (and animals) – sometimes, it must be said, to her own detriment.

It is fitting therefore, that Enid Blyton should have the last word. In reference to her beloved Isle of Purbeck, she wrote the poem *April Day*, where in the final verse she expresses not only her love of the place, but also the deep and abiding sense of spirituality which it evoked in her:

> Now let me stand and gaze –
>   But ah, so lavishly is beauty spread
> These April days,
>   There is no place to tread.
> Then must I choose
>   To put away my shoes
> And kneel instead.
>
> (From *April Day* by Enid Blyton)

NOTES

N.B. 'Famous Five' book references apply to the paperback series published individually, by Hodder Children's Books, excepting in the case of the two 'three in one' series – *Five on a Treasure Island/Five go Adventuring Again/Five go to Billycock Hill*; and *Five on a Secret Trail/Five go to Demon's Rock/Five have a Mystery to Solve* – by the same publisher.

Foreword
1.   Endecott, Vivienne, *The Dorset Days of Enid Blyton*, p.2.

Preface
1.   Baverstock, Gillian, *Gillian Baverstock remembers Enid Blyton*, p.29.

Chapter 1
1.   Blyton, Enid, in *Teacher's World*, 20 May, 1931.

Chapter 2
1.   Baverstock, Gillian, *Gillian Baverstock remembers Enid Blyton*, p.1.
2.   Stoney, Barbara, *Enid Blyton: The Biography*, p.16.
3.   Baverstock, op. cit., pp.3,7.
4.   Ibid, pp.9,4.
5.   Ibid, p.6.
6.   Ibid, p.8.
7.   Blyton, Enid, *The Story of My Life*, p.104.
8.   Stewart, Brian and Tony Summerfield, *The Enid Blyton Dossier*, p.9.
9.   Stoney, op. cit., pp.47-48,51,55.
10.   Baverstock, Gillian, to Dr A. Norman, 23 Mar. 2005.
11.   Baverstock, Gillian, *Gillian Baverstock remembers Enid Blyton*, p.10.
12.   Ibid, p.12.
13.   Blyton, Enid, *The Six Bad Boys*, p.89.
14.   Ibid, pp.67-68.
15.   Baverstock, Gillian, *Gillian Baverstock remembers Enid Blyton*, p.11.

Chapter 3
1.   Baverstock, Gillian, *Gillian Baverstock remembers Enid Blyton*, p.14.
2.   Baverstock, Gillian, to Dr A Norman, 23 Mar. 2005.
3.   Stoney, Barbara, *Enid Blyton: The Biography*, p.70.
4.   Baverstock, Gillian, *Gillian Baverstock remembers Enid Blyton*, p.16.
5.   Stewart, Brian and Tony Summerfield, *The Enid Blyton Dossier*, p.9.
6.   Stoney, op. cit., p.75.

7.   Stewart, Brian and Tony Summerfield, op.cit., p.83.
8.   Baverstock, Gillian, to Dr A. Norman, op. cit.

Chapter 4
1.   Stewart, Brian and Tony Summerfield, *The Enid Blyton Dossier*, p.85.
2.   Ibid, p.15.

Chapter 5
1.   Smallwood, Imogen, *A Childhood at Green Hedges*, p.49.
2.   Endecott, Vivienne, *The Dorset Days of Enid Blyton*, p.3.
3.   Smallwood, op. cit., p.59.

Chapter 6
1.   *Homeground*, BBC Film Documentary.
2.   Blyton, Enid, *Five on a Treasure Island*, p.126.
3.   Ibid, p.166.
4.   Endecott, Vivienne, *The Dorset Days of Enid Blyton*, p.5.

Chapter 7
1.   Blyton, Enid, *Five on a Treasure Island*, pp.49-50.
2.   The National Trust, *Corfe Castle, Dorset*, p.5.

Chapter 8
1.   Endecott, Vivienne, *The Dorset Days of Enid Blyton*, p.3.
2.   Meik, H.H., *The London and South Western Railway in Purbeck*, p.493.
3.   Clifford, David, *Swanage Railway Millennium Souvenir*, p.18.

Chapter 9
1.   Chacksfield, K. Merle, *Swanage at War*, pp.19-20.
2.   Ibid, p.27.
3.   Smallwood, Imogen, *A Childhood at Green Hedges*, p.86.
4.   Haysom, David and David Bragg, *Swanage and Purbeck in Old Photographs*, p.87.

Chapter 10
1.   Smale, Dennis, *The Rise and Fall of the Hotel Grosvenor*.
2.   Hardy, William Masters, *Old Swanage, or Purbeck Past and Present*, p.54.
3.   Smale, op. cit.
4.   Smallwood, Imogen, *A Childhood at Green Hedges*, p.218.
5.   Smale, op. cit.

Chapter 11
1.   Blyton, Enid, *Five on a Treasure Island*, p.24.

2.	Ibid, p.59.
3.	Hardy, William Masters, *Old Swanage, or Purbeck Past and Present*, p.33.
4.	W and R Dorset p.89; *Dorset Magazine* 1975 No.49 p.26; ST. 30.01.1875 (R): LR 1874-5 No. 247 (W).
5.	Blyton, Enid, to Col. A.D. Burnett Brown, 20 June 1952 and 24 June 1952.

Chapter 12
1.	Baverstock, Gillian, *Gillian Baverstock remembers Enid Blyton*, p.29.
2.	Blyton, Enid, *Five go to Smugglers' Top*, pp.21,28,33.
3.	Ibid, pp.53,64.
4.	Ibid, pp.83,174.

Chapter 13
1.	Saville, R.J., *A Langton Smuggler*, p.4.
2.	Ibid, p.9.
3.	Ibid, p.11.

Chapter 14
1.	Endecott, Vivienne, *The Dorset Days of Enid Blyton*, p.2.
2.	Smallwood, Imogen, *A Childhood at Green Hedges*, p.106.
3.	Endecott, op. cit., p.5.
4.	Baverstock, Gillian, *Gillian Baverstock remembers Enid Blyton*, p.30.
5.	Smallwood, op. cit., p.59.
6.	Endecott, op. cit., p.6.
7.	Baverstock, op. cit., p.26.
8.	Ibid, p.23.
9.	*Homeground,* BBC Film Documentary.
10.	Lewer, David, *The Story of Swanage*, p.17.
11.	Haysom, David and David Bragg, *Swanage and Purbeck in Old Photographs*, pp.12,18.

Chapter 15
1.	Blyton, Enid, *First Term at Malory Towers*, p.37.
2.	Ibid, p.4.
3.	Treves, Sir Frederick, *Highways and Byways in Dorset*, pp.195-96.

Chapter 16
1.	Blyton, Enid, *Five on Kirrin Island Again*, pp.1,18.
2.	Ibid, p.38.
3.	Ibid, p.117.
4.	Ibid, pp.185-186.
5.	Ibid, p.246.

Chapter 17
1. Blyton, Enid, *Five on Kirrin Island Again*, p.180.
2. Legg, Rodney, *Swanage Encyclopaedic Guide*, p.86.
3. Hardy, William Masters, *Old Swanage, or Purbeck Past and Present*, pp.20,21,9.

Chapter 18
1. Hardy, William Masters, *Old Swanage, or Purbeck Past and Present*, p.126.

Chapter 19
1. Smallwood, Imogen, *A Childhood at Green Hedges*, pp.27,100,105,114.
2. Ibid, p.116.
3. Greenfield, George, *Enid Blyton*, pp.58,59.
4. Stewart, Brian and Tony Summerfield, *The Enid Blyton Dossier*, p.90.

Chapter 20
1. Blyton, Enid, *Five Fall into Adventure*, pp.28,107

Chapter 21
1. Blyton, Enid, *The Rubadub Mystery*, pp.25,38,40,94,236.
2. Ibid, pp.145,147.
3. Ibid, pp.117,116.

Chapter 22
1. Endecott, Vivienne, *The Dorset Days of Enid Blyton*, p.5.
2. Popplewell, Lawrence, *Stoneblocks and Greenheart: Swanage seen from its Piers*. 1859-96, p.33.
3. Ibid, pp.63,92,69.

Chapter 23
1. Chacksfield, K. Merle, *100 Years of Golf on the Isle of Purbeck*, p.21.
2. Ibid, pp.34,43.
3. Ibid, pp.25-6.
4. *Homeground*, BBC Film Documentary.
5. Baverstock, Gillian, *Tell Me about Writers*, p.7.

Chapter 24
1. Blyton, Enid, *Five on a Treasure Island*. pp.11,13,14,22.
2. Blyton, Enid, *Five Have a Mystery to Solve*, pp.366,361.
3. Ibid, pp.363,393.

Chapter 25
1. Homeground BBC Film Documentary
2. The Dorset Police.

3.   Baverstock, Gillian, *Gillian Baverstock remembers Enid Blyton*, p.25.

Chapter 26
1.   Stoney, Barbara, *Enid Blyton: The Biography*, p.149.
2.   Chacksfield, K. Merle, *100 Years of Golf on the Isle of Purbeck*, p.76.
3.   Smallwood, Imogen, *A Childhood at Green Hedges*, p.145.

Chapter 27
1.   Endecott, Vivienne, *The Dorset Days of Enid Blyton*, p.2.
2.   Weinstock, M.B., *Old Dorset*, p.73.
3.   Information supplied by John Rowley.

Chapter 28
1.   Enid Blyton, *Five on a Secret Trail*, pp.69,72.
2.   Clark, Ronald W., *Sir Mortimer Wheeler*, pp.64-72.
3.   Blyton, Enid, *Adventure of the Strange Ruby*, p.13.
4.   Ibid, p.18.
5.   Ibid, p.19.
6.   Smallwood, Imogen, *A Childhood at Green Hedges*, p.146.

Chapter 29
1.   Blyton, Enid, *Five on Finniston Farm*, p.1.
2.   Ibid, pp.19,51.
3.   Ibid, pp.65,67.
4.   Ibid, pp.68,85.
5.   Ibid, p.97.
6.   *Homeground,* BBC Film Documentary.
7.   Royal Commission on Historical Monuments (England), *An Inventory of Historical Documents in the County of Dorset*, Vol.3, Part 2, pp.267,367.
8.   Hutchins, John, *The History and Antiquities of the County of Dorset*, Vol.III, p.667.
9.   Royal Commission on Historical Monuments (England), op. cit., Vol.3, Part 2, p.269.

Chapter 30
1.   Blyton, Enid, *Five go to Demon's Rocks*, pp.225,226,252.
2.   Lewer, David and Dennis Smale, *Swanage Past*, p.122.

Chapter 31
1.   Blyton, Enid, *Five have a Mystery to Solve*, p.370.
2.   Ibid, p.392.
3.   Ibid, p.395.
4.   Ibid, p.399.
5.   Ibid, p.478.

Chapter 32
1.   Bugler, John and Gregory Drew, *A History of Brownsea Island*, pp.38-9.
2.   Raalte, Charles van, *Brownsea Island*, pp.103-110.
3.   Bugler, op. cit., p.44.

Chapter 33
1.   Blyton, Enid, *The Story of My Life*, p.97.
2.   Baverstock, Gillian, to Dr A. Norman, 23 Mar. 2005.
3.   Smallwood, Imogen, *A Childhood at Green Hedges*, pp.90,49.
4.   Stewart, Brian and Tony Summerfield, *The Enid Blyton Dossier*, p.74.
5.   Smallwood, Imogen, op. cit., p.90.

Chapter 34
1.   Smallwood, Imogen, *A Childhood at Green Hedges*, p.149.
2.   Baverstock, Gillian, *Gillian Baverstock remembers Enid Blyton*, p.31.
3.   Smallwood, op. cit., p.149.
4.   Stoney, Barbara, *Enid Blyton: The Biography*, pp.182,183.
5.   Baverstock, op. cit., p.31.

Conclusion
1.   Blyton, Enid, to Kenneth McKeller, 15 Feb. 1953.
2.   Ibid.
3.   Blyton, Enid, to Kenneth McKellar, 26 Feb. 1953.
4.   Ibid.
5.   Blyton, Enid, *Five on Finniston Farm*, p.59.
6.   Blyton, Enid, to Kenneth McKellar, 26 Feb. 1953.

BIBLIOGRAPHY

Books and Publications

Battrick, Jack. 1978. *Brownsea Islander*. Poole, Dorset. Poole Historical Trust.

Baverstock, Gillian. 2000. *Gillian Baverstock remembers Enid Blyton*. London: Mammoth.

Baverstock, Gillian. 1997. *Tell Me about Writers*. London: Evans Brothers Ltd.

Blomfield, Richard. 1974. *Poole: Harbour, Heath and Island*. Sherborne, Dorset: Dorset Publishing Co.

Blue Pool, The. 1983. Derby: English Life Publications Ltd.

Blyton, Enid. 2000. *First Term at Malory Towers*. London: Mammoth.

Blyton, Enid. 1952. *The Story of My Life*. Norwich: Pitkin (Jarrold Publishing).

Blyton, Enid. 1942-63. The 'Famous Five' series of books. London: Hodder & Stoughton Ltd.

Blyton, Enid. 1951. *The Rubadub Mystery*. London: Award Publications Ltd.

Blyton, Enid. 1951. *The Six Bad Boys*. London: Lutterworth Press.

Brett, Susan. 1986. *A Dorset Wonderland*. Ringwood, Hampshire: Pleasure Books.

Bugler, John and Gregory Drew. 1995. *A History of Brownsea Island*. Dorchester, Dorset: Dorset County Library.

Chacksfield, K. Merle. 1993. *Swanage at War*. Swanage, Dorset: Swanage Town Council Leisure and Tourism Department.

Chacksfield, K. Merle. 1992. *100 Years of Golf on the Isle of Purbeck*. Isle of Purbeck Golf Club Ltd.

Clark, Ronald W. 1960. *Sir Mortimer Wheeler*. London: Phoenix House.

Clifford, David. 2000. *Swanage Railway Millennium Souvenir*. Dorchester, Dorset: Finial Publishing.

Davis, Terrence. 1984. *Wareham: Gateway to Purbeck*. Wincanton, Somerset: Dorset Publishing Company.

Dyson, Peter. 2000. *It Seems Like only Yesterday*. (In Swanage Railway Millennium Souvenir.)

Endecott, Vivienne. 2002. *The Dorset Days of Enid Blyton*. Poole, Dorset: Ginger Pop Productions.

Farrar, R.A.H. 1952. *Proceedings of the Dorset Natural History and Archaeological Society*. Vol.73. Dorchester: Longmans Ltd.

Greenfield, George. 1998. *Enid Blyton*. Stroud, Gloucs: Sutton Publishing.

Hardy, William Masters. 1910. *Old Swanage, or Purbeck Past and Present*. Dorchester: Dorset County Chronicle Printing Works.

Haysom, David and David Bragg. 1991. *Swanage and Purbeck in Old Photographs*. Stroud, Gloucs: Alan Sutton Publishing Ltd.

Hutchins, John. 1774. *The History and Antiquities of the County of Dorset*. Westminster: J.B. Nicholas & Sons.

Kidner, R.W. 2000. *The Railways of Purbeck*. Monmouthshire: The Oakwood Press.

Legg, Rodney. 1972. *Purbeck Island*. Wincanton, Somerset: Dorset Publishing Company.

Legg, Rodney. 1995. *Swanage Encyclopaedic Guide*. Wincanton, Somerset: Dorset Publishing Company.

Legg, Rodney. 2002. *The Book of Studland*. Tiverton, Devon: Halsgrove.

Lewer, David (ed.). 1990. *John Mowlem's Swanage Diary, 1845-1851*. Wincanton, Somerset: Dorset Publishing Company.

Lewer, David and Dennis Smale. 1994. *Swanage Past*. Chichester, Hampshire: Phillimore.

Lewer, David. 1986. *The Story of Swanage*. Bournemouth, UK: A Harewood Publication Visitors' Guide.

Lewer, David and J. Bernard Calkin. 1971. *Curiosities of Swanage, or Old London by the Sea*. Dorchester, Dorset: The Friary Press.

Lloyd, Rachel. 1967. *Dorset Elizabethans at Home and Abroad*. London: John Murray.

Mee, Arthur. 1959. *The King's England: Dorset*. London: Hodder and Stoughton Ltd.

Meik, H.H. 2000. *The London and South Western Railway in Purbeck*. (In Swanage Railway Millennium Souvenir.)

Morley, Geoffrey. 1983. *Smuggling in Hampshire and Dorset 1700-1850*. Newbury, Berkshire: Countryside Books.

Morris, Jeff. 1998. *The Story of the Swanage Lifeboats*.

National Trust, The. 1985. *Corfe Castle, Dorset*. The National Trust.

O'Hara, Mike and Ben Buxton. 2001. *Purbeck Camera*. Stanbridge, Wimborne, Dorset: Dovecote Press.

Pellatt, T. 1936. *Boys in the Making*. London: Methuen & Co. Ltd.

Popplewell, Lawrence. 1988. *Stoneblocks and Greenheart: Swanage seen from its Piers*. 1859-96. Southbourne, Dorset: Melledgen Press.

Raalte, Charles van. 1906. *Brownsea Island*. London: Arthur L. Humphreys.

Robinson, C.E. 1882. *Picturesque Rambles in the Isle of Purbeck*. London: The Typographic Etching Company.

Royal Commission on Historical Monuments (England). *An Inventory of*

Historical Documents in the County of Dorset. Vol.2. South-east. Part 1, and Vol.3. Central Dorset. Part 2. London.

Saville, R.J. 1976. *A Langton Smuggler.* Langton Matravers, Dorset. Langton Matravers Local History and Preservation Society. Booklet No.16.

Smale, Dennis. 2003. *The Rise and Fall of the Hotel Grosvenor.* [In *Dorset Life – The Dorset Magazine.*] Wareham, Dorset: The Dorset Magazine Ltd.

Smallwood, Imogen. 1989. *A Childhood at Green Hedges.* London: Methuen.

Star, The, Sheffield. 2 April 1988, Article, '*The Secret Life of Enid Blyton*'.

Stewart, Brian and Tony Summerfield. 1999. *The Enid Blyton Dossier.* Penryn, Cornwall: Hawk Books.

Stoney, Barbara. 1974. *Enid Blyton: The Biography.* London: Hodder and Stoughton Ltd.

Treves, Sir Frederick. 1906. *Highways and Byways in Dorset.* London: Wildwood House.

Weinstock, M.B. 1967. *Old Dorset.* Newton Abbot, Devon: David and Charles.

White, Allen. 1973. *Eighteenth Century Smuggling in Christchurch.* Christchurch, Dorset: Allen White.

Film Documentaries

Homeground. 2003. BBC South.